Healing Through Deliverance

Tom Brown

HEALING THROUGH DELIVERANCE

ISBN: 0-9740880-1-3

Published by

LIFEBRIDGE
BOOKS
P.O. BOX 49428
CHARLOTTE, NC 28277

Printed in the United States of America.
COVER DESIGN BY JR GRAPHICS

CONTENTS

INTRODUCTION

Millions saw it. Some were dumbfounded. Others skeptical. Still more were impressed.

The television camera zoomed in on Lori's face as the demon screamed through her voice, "No No! No!" She was writhing on her back, her hands swinging back and forth, punching, and grabbing as if someone else was pulling the strings.

Thirty-two-year old Lori appeared to be a normal person. She had a regular job and friends, but like many, she faced unbearable depression.

"I'm constantly depressed," she told the MSNBC reporters. She had been on medication, but was certain that demons were behind her disease. She had asked me, her pastor, to pray deliverance over her.

I did not want to start a circus. Deliverance is a personal matter, yet, at the same time, Jesus delivered people from demons in a public setting. So you can understand my reluctance and yet cautious willingness to allow the MSNBC television crew to film an actual deliverance. I did not want anyone embarrassed. I agreed to allow them in the service, provided anyone they filmed gave their written permission.

LOOKING FOR PROOF

Lori had agreed not only to be filmed, but also to be interviewed prior to the service. She told the reporters of the excruciating depression she had felt for years. She testified that strange, unexplainable marks were found on her body. The reporters saw the medication she had been taking. She was the ideal person they had looked for to do a documentary on exorcism. They wanted not just someone who claimed to be delivered from demons, but they wanted to verify the personal problems prior to the event, so they could either prove or disprove the value of deliverance. Lori agreed.

She came forward for prayer that Sunday morning. She stood on the platform, and all I could think to do was to point my finger at her and say, "I command you spirits to name yourselves in the name of Jesus Christ of Nazareth, the Son of God." Lori bowed her head, wrapped her arms around herself and began to sob uncontrollably. Soon she was prostrate on the floor sobbing even louder.

Lori bowed her head, wrapped her arms around herself and began to sob uncontrollably.

I felt I knew which spirits were in her. "I command all thoughts of suicide, all thoughts of lust, anger, bitterness, and self pity, to come out! You will all come out. I called you by name."

THE RESULTS

Soon, Lori was calmed. A wide grin spread across her

olive-skin face. She was freed. The deliverance was over in five minutes. Afterward she described to the reporters what it felt like: "It was the most unusual thing I have ever experienced."

She did not feel in control during the whole session. The important thing, however, was the results. Over the watchful, scrutinizing eyes of the MSNBC reporters, they admitted after two days of Lori's deliverance that she was not depressed.

"I don't have to take pills. I can handle everyday problems," Lori was delighted to say.

Since her freedom Lori has been a faithful member of our church, and is serving the Lord with all her heart. (Of course, as in all cases of deliverance, there is no guarantee of permanent results, since Jesus warned that spirits might come back to make the person worse [see Matthew 12:43-45].)

Toward the end of the documentary, MSNBC admitted that some people seem to get better following deliverance. Psychologists may attribute the success to psychological release, hypnotism, or just positive faith on the part of the individual. Hopefully more professionals will applaud the efforts of ministers like myself who are attempting to help people get rid of their demons through the word of God and prayer.

WHAT THIS BOOK WILL DO FOR YOU

Since the televised documentary I have received many calls, letters and emails from people around the world asking for deliverance. Many simply have questions concerning exorcism and demons.

After the airing of this program I appeared on national

television and have been interviewed on a wide-range of questions regarding this subject. Even the British Broadcasting Company has interviewed me about exorcism. With many requests for prayer and the desire of individuals to find answers about deliverance, I have decided to write a book on this subject.

You will learn Satan's number one trap and how you can avoid it.

On these pages I have attempted to answer questions on this topic and to provide sound, logical and scriptural teaching as to the scope and value of deliverance. I hope this information will strengthen your faith and help you live a victorious life in Christ Jesus.

- You will learn how to tell the difference between natural sickness and demonic sickness.
- You will discover what a generational curse is, how it can bring affliction into your life, and more importantly, how to break it.
- You will acquire the knowledge necessary concerning yourself, and what it means for you to be a spirit, soul and body – and how this relates to Satan's attacks.
- You will recognize the works of Satan and how to stop him.
- You will find out what the occult is and how it can subtly induce you to the realm of the spirits of darkness.
- You will learn Satan's number one trap and how you can avoid it.

- You will be challenged to have your own ministry of deliverance.
- You will be inspired with real stories of people that received their healing through deliverance.

HOW THE BOOK IS ARRANGED

The volume is divided into four sections. The first three sections cover the three compartments of health – physical, mental and spiritual. I want you to see the need to be healed in all three domains, and understand the ways demons can make people sick in those areas.

The fourth section deals with common objections people raise concerning the ministry of deliverance. I make an important defense for the need to have both a power encounter and a truth encounter, if people are going to be helped by the ministry of deliverance. This section concludes with stories of real people from our church that received their healing when they were delivered from evil spirits.

I encourage you to read your Bible along with this book. This is not about my views but what I honestly believe God's Word teaches about deliverance. You can look up the references yourself and check to verify whether or not the scriptures really say what I quote them as saying. I have nothing to hide. If what I write is not based on scripture, then challenge me! Of course you will have to challenge me with scriptures since my belief is derived only from the Bible.

I understand that many do not believe in the Bible, so they will find this book irrelevant. For others, however, scripture is their source of authority. Wisely, they will compare the teaching contained on these pages with the

Word of God.

I pray this book provides the answers and scriptural knowledge you desire. More important, it is my utmost longing that you will receive the healing you need – that oftentimes can come *only* through deliverance.

– *Tom Brown*

PART I

PHYSICAL DISEASES

CHAPTER 1

THE ROLE OF DEMONS AND SICKNESS

On a Sabbath, Jesus was teaching in one of the synagogues. A woman was there who had been crippled by a spirit for eighteen years.

She was bent over and could not straighten up at all. When Jesus saw her, he called her forward and said to her, "Woman, you are set free from your infirmity." Then he put his hands on her, and immediately she straightened up and praised God. Indignant because Jesus had healed on the Sabbath, the synagogue ruler said to the people, "There are six days for work. So come and be healed on those days, not on the Sabbath." The Lord answered him, "You hypocrites! Doesn't each of you on the Sabbath untie his ox or donkey from the stall and lead it out to give it water? Then should not this woman, a daughter of Abraham, whom Satan has kept bound for eighteen long years, be set free on the Sabbath day from what bound her?" (Luke 13:10-16).

On another occasion, a man knelt before Jesus, saying, *"Lord, have mercy on my son," he said. "He has seizures and is suffering greatly. He often falls into the fire or into the water. I brought him to your disciples, but they could not heal him." "O unbelieving and perverse generation," Jesus replied, "how long shall I stay with you? How long shall I put up with you? Bring the boy here to me." Jesus rebuked the demon, and it came out of the boy, and he was healed from that moment* (Matthew 17:15-18).

WHAT IS THE CAUSE?

There is a definite relationship between healing and the need for deliverance. In my travels around the world I have discovered that many are never healed because they have never received deliverance from the spirits that made them sick. I am not saying that every disease is caused by a demon. There is a need for both natural healing and demonic healing.

There is a need for both natural healing and demonic healing.

That evening after sunset the people brought to Jesus all the sick and demon-possessed. The whole town gathered at the door, and Jesus healed many who had various diseases. He also drove out many demons, but he would not let the demons speak because they knew who he was (Mark 1:32-34).

Notice that Jesus accomplished two things: *Jesus healed many who had various diseases* and *He also drove out many demons.*

Some people simply need healing from the *diseases* that have made them sick; others need deliverance from the *spirits* that have caused an infirmity. Just the thought that demons could be behind sickness sounds radical. If that is the case, then perhaps we need a radical approach to healing.

Some people might caution me at this point and say, "Pastor Tom, we need balance."

I agree. I believe in balance, however, to some people the word means a middle of the road compromise. Yet, that is not how Jesus achieved balance. The Lord attained it by being extreme in all points. Jesus taught:

- Extreme love – "Turn the other cheek."
- Extreme holiness – "If your right eye sins, gouge it out."
- Extreme faith – "If you have faith as a mustard seed you can speak to a mountain."
- Extreme evangelism – "Go into all the world and preach the gospel."
- Extreme deliverance – "In my name you shall drive out demons."

Balance is not achieved by watering down the fundamentals of the Christian faith. If we do that we will have a lukewarm Christianity, and I think people are tired of tepid faith.

The Bible provides a radical approach to healing as far as modern thinking is concerned – including the thinking of born again believers.

Many Christians quote C. S. Lewis, "Don't ignore the devil or give him too much attention." I agree. But does this mean we ignore the role demons may play regarding sickness? I don't think so.

During the 1960s, when the deliverance movement was at its peek, many Christians saw demons behind every bush.

It seemed that any problem someone had was attributed to a demon – from the flu to overeating. Now, with such a de-emphasis on the devil and demons by the Church, you no longer have to look behind the shrubbery for demons; you can find them parading down the streets almost unnoticed.

When was the last time you went to a Christian conference where they had a seminar speaker devoted to the teaching of deliverance?

Today pastors, evangelists, and prophets teach on church growth, friendly evangelism, prosperity, and a host of other important subjects. Rarely do they mention deliverance.

"How can you tell if a demon is the cause of the sickness?"

Don't misunderstand me. I believe in teaching all these needed subjects, but how about devoting a portion of the seminars to the scriptural principles of setting people free. The problem with this de-emphasis of demons is not just found in ecclesiastical and denominational churches, it can be encountered in Pentecostal and Charismatic churches as well.

The Spirit-filled movement seems to be afraid to tackle this subject, perhaps because they don't want to be viewed as unscientific or they are afraid that Christians will give disproportionate time to demons. Whatever the case, I believe we need a new and greater emphasis on deliverance, with a stress on biblical accuracy.

IS IT THE DEVIL?

I am often asked, "How can you tell if a demon is the source of the sickness or if it is just a natural cause?" This is a great question, and I have diligently searched the scriptures to come up with some answers.

Here are ten ways I have been able to know whether or not demons are behind a sickness:

1. **It is demonic if the discernings of spirits is in operation.**

But to each one is given the manifestation of the Spirit to profit withal. For to one is given through the Spirit the word of wisdom; and to another the word of knowledge, according to the same Spirit: to another faith, in the same Spirit; and to another gifts of healings, in the one Spirit; and to another workings of miracles; and to another prophecy; and to another discernings of spirits; to another (divers) kinds of tongues; and to another the interpretation of tongues (1 Corinthians 12:7-10 ASV).

Notice the seventh gift on the list: *discernings of spirits.* God gives at times the ability to see and perceive the operation of good and evil spirits.

The word *discernings* comes from the word "judge." It is hard at times to judge whether a spirit is the cause of a sickness, but through the gifting of the Holy Spirit you will be able to correctly decide.

The word *discernings* is actually in the plural, and this is how it is in the original Greek. This means that discernment can come in various forms. For example, it can arrive in the form of a *vision*, in which you actually see the demon with your eyes.

One of the most influential charismatic leaders, Kenneth Hagin, tells the story of when he was preaching in a country church and a man came forward for prayer. From every outward appearance he appeared normal, except his face showed pain. As he came closer to the preacher, Hagin said he had a vision in which he saw a monkey-looking creature wrapping his arms around the man's head, as in a headlock. Immediately, brother Hagin exclaimed to the spirit, "In the name of Jesus, you foul spirit, leave this man at once!"

The spirit looked startled and taken back that Hagin had seen him. Next, the spirit eyed him for a moment, so Hagin said to him again, looking him in the eyes, "I told you to leave this man!"

Knowing that the spirit had been uncovered, it replied, "Well, I don't want to leave, but if you tell me I have to, then I'll go."

With boldness, Hagan commanded, "You *will* have to go." The spirit released the man's head and jumped off his shoulders, landing on the floor. It just looked at Hagin for a moment.

Hagin persisted, "You will have to leave the premises now!" The spirit whimpered like a beaten dog, and stumbled out of the church.

This story is a dramatic account of the discernings of spirits coming in the form of a vision. I personally have not experienced any visions of demons, but I have had the discernings of spirits work in other ways.

The word "discern" means to perceive by the *sight* or some *other sense* or by the *intellect*. As you can tell from this definition, discernment is not perception by *sight* only, it can come through other senses, such as hearing, smelling or feeling.

Oral Roberts, the renown healing evangelist, says that oftentimes he can *smell* the demon in a person. Perhaps no one else can smell it at the time, but he can. This is another form of discernment.

Many *feel* the presence of a demon. They may start to sweat, become clammy, or have a tingling sensation.

I have heard some say they feel fire when they get near a demon. Hagin was told by the Lord that when he lays both hands on the sick, if he feels fire going back and forth between his hands then there is a presence of a demon in the sick person he is praying for. Others may feel cold, a chill or some physical sensation. God is sovereign, so He will work with you in His way to help you discern a demon.

Many feel the presence of a demon. They may start to sweat, become clammy, or have a tingling sensation.

The more common way that discernment works, however, is through a "knowing" that something is there. You may call it your *intellect* or gut feeling. You just "know that you know" that a spirit is behind a sickness. This is another form of discernment and this is the typical way God speaks to me in these situations.

2. It is demonic if there are no natural causes of the illness.

A telltale sign that a demon may be the one inducing the sickness is when there is no natural explanation for the condition. Sometimes this kind of sickness is called "psychosomatic." It is believed that something in the person's mind is causing the symptoms. Many discount this type of illness. However, if the person is suffering pain or symptoms (even if you cannot pinpoint the cause), the individual is still hurting and needs healing.

I believe some psychosomatic illnesses are caused by demons, and this explains why doctors can't uncover the cause. You cannot spot a demon on x-rays; you cannot see one in a blood sample. Demons are not perceptible through science and modern methods of investigation.

In such cases, I have found great success in bringing healing through deliverance. The number one reason people suffer psychosomatic illness is due to stress. (We will discuss this later in Chapter Eight.)

3. It is demonic if the disease is chronic and should normally have been cured.

One of the great powers of the human body is its ability to heal itself. For example, when you cut yourself, the body immediately begins to heal the cut: it sends bacteria- fighting agents, forms a scab for protection, and eventually the scab falls off and the body is well. This is normal.

I believe some chronic conditions are demonic, and this is why they linger.

Consider what happens if there is an evil spirit that is the cause of the infirmity. How then can the body heal itself? It can't heal naturally when there is an evil spirit present.

Chronic illnesses are usually permanent – the malady stays with you. I believe some chronic conditions are demonic, and this is why they linger. No matter how hard the body tries to fight off the illness it can't, because the demon enforces the disease. In cases like this the afflicting spirit must be driven out.

The first scripture at the beginning of this chapter deals with the woman who was *crippled by a spirit for eighteen years.* It is not normal for the body to stay crippled. If a bone breaks it usually heals. In this case, her backbones began to form improperly, and the condition never corrected itself. She remained like this for eighteen years – a chronic illness. The Bible says it was caused by a *spirit.*

If it appears that the person should have recovered from the disease, yet hasn't, then I deal with the evil spirit and drive it from the person.

4. It is demonic if the sickness affects the spiritual life of the sick.

Demons, when they are present, do not just affect the body but also the spiritual life of the individual.

Do the infirmed have peace even though they are sick? If they feel totally at ease, even when afflicted, then most likely the disease is natural. There is probably no demon involved.

I often look to find evidence of spiritual growth. If it is occurring in the sick person, their disease seems to be of natural causes. On the other hand, if the sick are being hurt spiritually, then the disease could have some demonic roots.

Demons are not interested in simply bringing physical infirmities, they desire to hurt the spiritual life of the person.

Once I was speaking in a small church in the suburbs of Dallas. I preached my heart out, yet there was very little enthusiastic response from the congregation, except for one dear elderly woman who kept shouting, "Praise the Lord!

That's right! Keep preaching!" She was so exuberant.

After the service, while I was signing my books, a rather large gentleman walked up to me and said, "I want to apologize for my mother. She was the one who kept shouting 'Praise the Lord.'"

I told him not to worry, that I *enjoyed* her enthusiastic response. Then he told me, "You see, she shouts praises because she has Alzheimer's." The only person who seemed to enjoy the message was a lady with Alzheimer's!

Here is my point: this dear woman did not have a demon. A demon would not be shouting, "Praise the Lord!" Her disease was physical. She was still intact spiritually even though her mind was diseased.

On the other hand, I have seen physically ill people become *furious* at my preaching. Who would get upset over the ministry of the Word? The only ones would be the devil and his demons.

If you are physically sick, give yourself a checkup. For example, if you find yourself becoming angry over reading this book or listening to the gospel being preached, could it be you are not only sick in body, but there is also something else wrong?

Many Christians grow spiritually during their sickness, and that is an indication they don't have a demon. However, in cases where they are not experiencing spiritual growth, rather they are becoming bitter, angry, and more sinful, then I believe that their sickness has a demonic root. They need more than healing; they need deliverance

5. It is demonic if there are strange occurrences taking place with the disease.

A danger sign there are demons causing the infirmity is

when there are unusual happenings taking place with the person who is sick.

In the introduction to this book I mentioned Lori, who suffered from depression. How was she convinced it was a spirit that caused her condition? She knew it because she also had strange, unexplained marks on her body.

How was she convinced it was a spirit that caused her condition?

Lori did not just suffer from clinical depression; there was something else tormenting her. Those marks on her body testified that there were supernatural agents involved in her condition.

Here is a scripture to consider: *"Lord, have mercy on my son," he said. "He has seizures and is suffering greatly. He often falls into the fire or into the water"...Jesus rebuked the demon, and it came out of the boy, and he was healed from that moment* (Matthew 17:15,18).

How can we tell the boy's problem wasn't simply epileptic seizures? In this case, we can know by the fact that the attacks took place at very inopportune times, especially at moments that endangered the boy's life. He would have the seizures near fire or water, and would often *fall into* them. That was a sign of demons.

This also happens today. Some people become ill at the most inappropriate times, such as when they go to church or attend a very important meeting. I have successfully prayed deliverance for people who seem to get sick only on Sunday mornings and at no other time. It is clear that the devil is causing the infirmity to occur at certain moments in order to prevent the person from hearing the Word. Others become sick when they start to read the Bible, while some fall ill when they begin to share their faith.

In the case with epilepsy, we need to ask: does the person have seizures at very dangerous times or at ordinary times? If the attacks usually come during unsafe times, it appears that demons may be the cause. However, if the seizures take place at normal times then it is likely to be a physical problem only.

Someone might ask, "If the disease is diagnosed by doctors, doesn't that disprove that demons are causing the sickness?"

Not really, because there is a false assumption that diseases have life in themselves, and that no spirit is causing the disease to live. For example, the Bible says, "The body without the spirit is dead." Although you cannot see the human spirit, it is the force that keeps the body alive. Doctors might think it is the heart that sustains life. Yet the Bible says it is the *spirit* that gives us breath.

Just as an invisible force keeps our bodies functioning, the same is true of diseases.

Just as an invisible force keeps our bodies functioning, the same is true of diseases.

A disease may have some life beyond the germ that keeps it alive. The condition is real and can be seen; yet the evil spirit behind the disease may keep it alive, just as our human spirit keeps our bodies alive.

Once the offending spirit is cast out of the body, then the disease – without its life source – must die. This is why an illness may have both physical and demonic roots.

6. It is demonic if the person becomes strangely ill or emotionally distraught when an anointed person is in their presence.

So they brought [the boy to Jesus]. When the spirit saw Jesus, it immediately threw the boy into a convulsion. He fell to the ground and rolled around, foaming at the mouth (Mark 9:20).

Notice that the boy convulsed as soon as *the spirit saw Jesus.*

I have watched people become physically and emotionally ill the moment they are in my presence. They can't understand it. Some get nauseated, others become depressed or terribly afraid. Those afflicted with demons will often refuse prayer or feel very uncomfortable when people pray for them.

A person may be seriously ill, but instead of turning to a minister for help, they often despise the man or woman of God. This is a clear indication that demons are involved with those individuals.

Another related symptom I have seen is when mentally ill people become very angry and nervous around me. I have seen these people scream in the service. They cry out, "I want to leave! Get me out of here!" Evidently, God's anointing resting on me torments the demons inside of them.

This is what happened in the case with Jesus. The demon threw the boy to the ground once it saw the Lord.

At times people fall down when they get close to an anointed minister. Often they become prostrate in God's presence, but at other times the cause is an evil spirit.

You can tell which spirit has caused them to fall by looking at the results when they are on the floor. Do they look peaceful and joyful; or are they writhing, growling, and screaming? Unfortunately, many do not have the discernment to tell the difference.

It has been reported to me that in some religious circles, if people bark like dogs, they are considered really touched by the Lord. Come on! Aren't we smarter than that? Such signs should make it obvious that demons are causing the individuals to act that way. Yet, many ministers leave these people alone and attribute such weird acts to the Holy Spirit.

We need to obey the scripture that says, *"Test the spirits to see whether they are from God"* (1 John 4:1).

7. It is demonic if the sick become extremely homesick when they leave town.

For Jesus had said to him, "Come out of this man, you evil spirit!" Then Jesus asked him, "What is your name?" "My name is Legion," he replied, "for we are many." And he begged Jesus again and again not to send them out of the area (Mark 5:8-10).

The demon pleaded with Jesus repeatedly not to send them out of the area. Evil spirits prefer to stay in the same location if possible, for whatever reason. A possible explanation may have something to do with rank and territory.

Paul mentions four classifications of evil spiritual entities in Ephesians 6: rulers, authorities, powers and forces. These were common military terms in his day. It appears that demons must answer to higher-ranking demons. They do not want to leave the area without proper demonic authority, because they might feel like they are AWOL, and do not want to be disciplined by other spirits higher than themselves. This is only my speculation, but one thing for sure, as this story illustrates, they do not like to leave their territory.

This brings us to another sign of demonic activity with the sick. Since demons prefer to stay in certain locations, the demonically afflicted may find themselves unable to leave their home or city. They become very homesick when they do. This may be caused by the demons that do not want to leave the area.

It is not typical to want to stay at home all the time. We are creatures of adventure. It is normal and healthy to get out of the house and even travel out of town.

Do you have trouble leaving your house or city? Do you find yourself homesick soon after you depart, or are you even hesitant to take a vacation? You might even turn down employment opportunities because you don't want to move from your present location. Of course, if you have a good church and family in your city that is understandable, but others do not have any legitimate reasons for turning down promotions, except some inexplicable urge to stay where they are; they are often also troubled with sickness. This is a warning sign of demonic infirmities.

Since demons prefer to stay in certain locations, the demonically afflicted may find themselves unable to leave their home or city.

8. It is demonic if the infirmity returns after being healed.

When an evil spirit comes out of a man, it goes through arid places seeking rest and does not find it. Then it says, '" I will return to the house I left." When it arrives, it finds the house unoccupied, swept clean and put in order. Then it goes and takes with it seven other spirits more wicked than itself, and they go in and live there. And the final condition of that man is worse than the first. That is how it will be with this wicked generation (Matthew 12:43-45).

Jesus taught that demons would attempt to come back. A sign of a disease with demonic origins is when it *returns.* If a disease is healed then it is unlikely to reoccur.

The odds are extremely low for the same condition to comeback. However, an evil spirit makes every attempt to return – and bring back the disease that was healed.

When this happens, I usually look for the demon behind the infirmity and cast it out.

9. It is demonic if a worse sickness replaces the one that was healed.

Jesus said, *And the final condition of that man is worse than the first* (Matthew 12:45).

There have been people who are healed from one condition only to later become sick with an illness far more severe. They might even recover from that disease, and find another infirmity comes upon them, which is even worse.

In such cases, something is desperately wrong. The individual seems to never stay well. It should be obvious that something abnormal is occurring. The person should definitely seek deliverance.

10. It is demonic if the disease is hereditary and can be proven that the previous generation practiced idolatry.

In the next chapter we will discuss in detail when a disease is hereditary. If it can be proven that the previous generation practiced idolatry then demons may be inducing the sickness.

SEEK GOD

These are possible ways to judge whether or not physical diseases are caused by demons or if they are natural. You do not necessarily have to experience everything I mentioned in this chapter, however, if you have a symptom that fits the biblical criteria of demonic sickness, then take the matter to God in prayer.

Only the Father is authorized to show you whether or not you have a "spirit of infirmity." If He confirms it to you, then keep on reading. Help is on the way!

CHAPTER 2

THE GENERATIONAL CURSE

Mary had just returned from the doctor. It was confirmed; her worst suspicions and fears had come true. "I'm sorry to tell you, but the cyst is cancerous," her doctor said as he peered through his horn-rimed bifocals.

She knew it before the doctor had told her. Cancer had run in her family. Her mother had died of it, her older sister, Sofia, was being treated for it, and now it was her turn.

It just didn't seem fair! Mary complained. *Other women were never going to get cancer, simply because they had different parents.* Mary's situation parallels many others.

Hereditary diseases are common. Research is proving that genetics play a major part in one's good health – or lack of it. Does it seem unfair that one should inherit a negative trait from their parents? Actually the idea of inheriting blessings and curses from our parents is thoroughly scriptural. Consider the most far-reaching generational curse to ever come upon the human race – Adam and us.

For just as through the disobedience of the one man the many were made sinners, so also through the obedience of the one man the many will be made righteous (Romans 5:19).

We inherit the "sin nature" from Adam.

We receive the "sin nature" from Adam. We may not like the fact, but it is true nevertheless. Consequently, we suffer under the curse that befell the original man.

If God had not made provision for us to be free from the curses of our ancestors, this would not be fair. Yet He did. Jesus is the answer.

REDEEMED! REDEEMED!

Consider the cross. It is both vertical and horizontal. The vertical speaks of our relationship with God and the horizontal represents our relationship with people. The cross redeems us from any curse that may attempt to attach itself, whether the condemnation is the judgment from God or a result of the sin of others. *Christ has redeemed us from the curse* (Galatians 3:13).

What is the cause? Sin. It's that simple! Read Deuteronomy chapter 28. There God warns Israel that if they break His commandments, they would be under a curse.

However, if you do not obey the Lord your God and do not carefully follow all his commands and decrees I am giving you today, all these curses will come upon you and overtake you: You will be cursed in the city and cursed in the country. Your basket and your kneading trough will be cursed. The fruit of your womb will be cursed, and the crops of your land, and the calves of your herds and the lambs of your flocks. You will be cursed when you come in and cursed when you go out. (Deuteronomy 28:15-19).

Notice how often God mentions the word "cursed." This may seem superstitious to the modern mind. Some think curses do not exist, but they do!

God's wrath, however, does not come without reason. *Like a fluttering sparrow or a darting swallow, an undeserved curse does not come to rest* (Proverbs 26:2).

Curses must be deserved, or they do not rest on anyone. The King James version presents the passage in these words: *As the bird by wandering, as the swallow by flying, so the curse causeless shall not come.* This tells us there must be a *cause* for the curse. Let me repeat: the reason for curses is iniquity.

THE SIN OF IDOLATRY

One particular transgression is very offensive to God and extremely dangerous to your life and the lives of your children. What is that sin?

The Almighty declares, *You shall not make for yourself an idol in the form of anything in heaven above or on the earth beneath or in the waters below. You shall not bow down to them or worship them; for I, the Lord your God, am a jealous God, punishing the children for the sin of the fathers to the third and fourth generation of those who hate me, but showing love to a thousand of those who love me and keep my commandments* (Exodus 20:4-6).

Breaking the second commandment is so abhorrent to God that it brings a curse on the offender and their children, even up to four generations. None of the other Ten Commandments carry this curse. Why this particular one? Why is the sin of idolatry so offensive that there is a curse placed on the individual and his descendants? We will answer that question in this chapter.

What is idolatry? It is *worshiping idols.* An idol is a representative of a god – an image or likeness.

Question: Is there more than one God? Of course not,

there is only *one.* Then what are the so-called gods? In writing to the Corinthians, Paul gives the answer. *Do I mean then that a sacrifice offered to an idol is anything, or that an idol is anything? No, but the sacrifices of pagans are offered to demons, not to God, and I do not want you to be participants with demons* (1 Corinthians 10:20).

The apostle tells us that an idol is nothing. It is really not a god nor does it represent a true deity. Then he makes a startling revelation: he states that an idol is a demon. This is extremely important to understand. When a person worships or pays homage to an idol, whether they realize it or not, they are actually worshiping a demon.

Paul did not pull this revelation out of his hat; he actually received this teaching in the Hebrew scriptures: *They made him jealous with their foreign gods and angered him with their detestable idols. They sacrificed to demons, which are not God – gods they had not known, gods that recently appeared, gods your fathers did not fear* (Deuteronmy 32:16-17).

There is the proof! Idols are demons.

TO THE NEXT GENERATION

Since we have discovered what idols truly are, how does this relate to a curse being placed on the idolater's family? To answer this, we must go to the New Testament and look at the teachings that Jesus gave concerning demons.

When an evil spirit comes out of a man, it goes through arid places seeking rest and does not find it. Then it says, "I will return to the house I left." When it arrives, it finds the house unoccupied, swept clean and put in order. Then it goes and takes with it seven other spirits more wicked than itself, and they go in and live there. And the final condition of that man is worse than the first. That is how it will be with this wicked generation (Matthew 12:43-45).

Notice that Jesus said when a demon leaves a person, it tries to come back and bring other spirits worse than itself. Then Jesus added, *That is how it will be with this wicked generation.* Jesus' conclusion is unmistakable: the *wicked generation* in His day was a result of evil spirits coming from the parents.

The word for "generation" is *genea*, and we take our word "gene" from this Greek word.

What happens to a demon when the person dies?

Jesus was telling the people that their genes had come from wicked parents who had worshiped demons, and now they remained in their families – and had brought *more* evil spirits with them. As a result, the demons made them more sinful than their parents.

Let me ask you this question: what happens to a demon when the person dies? Is the demon buried with the deceased? Of course not! It continues on the earth and is transferred to the children. This is how the generational curse works. It comes in the form of an evil spirit (when such a spirit is invited into a person's life through idolatry), then continues in that genealogical line. This will explain how the children are punished through their parent's sin.

Another proof that demons stay in the family is in the actual name of a demon. A common Old Testament designation for a demon is *"familiar spirit"* (Deuteronomy 18:11).The Spanish word for family – *familia* – is similar. The Hebrew word is 'owb (pronounced *obe*), and conveys the same thought. *Strong's Concordance* says that it carries the idea of prattling (or babbling) a father's name. The demon chatters the name of the father as his entitlement to be there. As you can see, a familiar spirit is a "family" spirit.

The Greed Factor

Most people from educated backgrounds feel secure. They can't imagine anyone in their family ever committing idolatry. However, there is another form of this sin that many, especially educated people, commit. The kind of idolatry I am talking about is greed.

For of this you can be sure: No immoral, impure or greedy person – such a man is an idolater – has any inheritance in the kingdom of Christ and of God (Ephesians 5:5).

Who is an idolater? According to this scripture, it is a *greedy* person. Wow! Most think of idolaters as pagans in third world countries where they practice voodoo. They can't imagine such a person living in Manhattan and a member of the New York Stock Exchange. The Word of God, however, expands on our understanding. It includes every segment of society – from the obvious idolaters to the not so obvious.

There is both overt and covert idolatry. Regardless of which category a person may fall into, it is the same sin.

Greed brings a curse on your children. *With eyes full of adultery, they never stop sinning; they seduce the unstable; they are experts in greed – an accursed brood!* (2 Peter 2:14).

Greed is idolatry.

The word *brood* is an outdated term we seldom use. Jesus, however, used the word frequently. He called the religious leaders, *"You brood of vipers!"* (Matthew 3:7).

It derives from the word *blood.* Notice how similar the spelling is. Just replace the "r" with "l". The word brood means *bad blood.* The King James says they are "cursed children."

What Will We Inherit?

Modern medicine has recently discovered the unique

relationship of genetics and health. They can often predict whether children are likely to become ill based on the health of the parents. They know how the blood contains the genetic makeup of each individual. We inherit the genes from our parents. According to scripture, if their blood is cursed, then we can inherit their cursed genes.

We see this in the life of Gehazi – the apprentice of prophet Elisha. After healing Naaman, Elisha was offered money, but the prophet turned it down. Elisha wanted to make a strong impact on this pagan officer, so he did not want money to stand in the way of converting him and the nation he served.

Gehazi, however, felt differently. He said to himself, "My master let this man off too easily." Then Gehazi went after Naaman and told him that Elisha would accept some money for his friends that had just come to visit him. After taking the funds, Gehazi hid the money in his tent.

The Bible records, *Then [Gehazi] went in and stood before his master Elisha. "Where have you been, Gehazi?" Elisha asked. "Your servant didn't go anywhere," Gehazi answered. But Elisha said to him, "Was not my spirit with you when the man got down from his chariot to meet you? Is this the time to take money, or to accept clothes, olive groves, vineyards, flocks, herds, or menservants and maidservants? Naaman's leprosy will cling to you and to your descendants forever." Then Gehazi went from Elisha's presence and he was leprous, as white as snow* (II Kings 5:25-27).

It is clear that Gehazi was greedy, and here was his punishment: he would inherit Naaman's leprosy, but not just him, also his children. Gehazi operated in *greed* which is idolatry. This opened the door to demons, that remained in his family.

Gehazi's children inherited demons – through which come generational curses.

CHAPTER 3

HOW TO BREAK THE CURSE

You may say, "It is not fair to be judged for my parents' sin."

That is true. As we will learn, the Lord will *not* judge you for the transgressions of your parents. When God delivered the Ten Commandments, He declared that we should not bow down to any graven image, *...for I the Lord thy God am a jealous God, visiting the iniquity of the fathers upon the children unto the third and fourth generation of them that hate me* (Exodus 20:5 KJV).

The iniquity would not come to any children, but to those who *hate* God. This is confirmed by the Lord through the prophet Ezekiel. *For every living soul belongs to me, the father as well as the son – both alike belong to me. The soul who sins is the one who will die* (Ezekiel 18:4).

This scripture establishes that every person is accountable for his own actions – and will not be held responsible for his father's transgressions.

Ezekiel then gives an illustration concerning a sinful

father and a righteous son. *But suppose this son has a son who sees all the sins his father commits, and though he sees them, he does not do such things....He will not die for his father's sin; he will surely live...Yet you ask, "Why does the son not share the guilt of his father?" Since the son has done what is just and right and has been careful to keep all my decrees, he will surely live. The soul who sins is the one who will die. The son will not share the guilt of the father, nor will the father share the guilt of the son* (Ezekiel 18:14,17-20).

IT'S NOT AUTOMATIC!

The prophet was not contradicting what God said about punishing the children, because the Lord declared they would be chastised only if they *hated* Me. In other words, if they continued down the same path as their parents then they would also be punished. The generational curse is not automatic; it may be broken! It is not required to fall on anyone.

The generational curse is not automatic; it may be broken.

Unfortunately, experience tells us that children often follow the life patterns of their parents. It is common to see similar behaviors in a family – alcoholism, obesity, teenage pregnancy, worry, anger, abusiveness to wives and children, divorce, gambling, laziness, adultery, crime, and more.

FATHERS AND SONS

The Bible gives examples of sons following in the footsteps of the father. Consider the first murderer in the

Bible: Cain. After he killed his brother, what happened to his descendants? Four generations later, Lamech laments to his wives, *I have killed a man for wounding me, a young man for injuring me. If Cain is avenged seven times, then Lamech seventy-seven times* (Genesis 4:23).

He followed his great, great grandfather and experienced a curse ten times greater than Cain's.

Look at Abraham and Isaac. Abraham gave his wife to Pharaoh for fear of losing his life. Later, Isaac does the same thing when confronted with fear. He offered his wife, Rebekah, to the King just like his father. (Compare Genesis 20:2 and 26:7) Again and again we see children imitating their parents.

Repeating the Pattern

I was teaching this message to a group of prisoners. Out of the seventy men present, I asked for a show of hands of the men who were simply repeating the awful behavior they saw in at least one of their parents. Sixty-five of the men raised their hands. Only five said that they were the prodigal sons who abandoned the godly lifestyle of their fathers. The great majority of men incarcerated are not the black sheep of the family, they are *representatives* of their families.

Children cannot expect to be exempt from the generational curse if they continue in the wicked ways of their parents. We are fooling ourselves if we expect to have the curse broken, yet do not want to repent.

What Will Happen?

According to scripture, curses come in many forms. We are told that even *The fruit of your womb will be cursed*

(Deuteronomy 28:18).

Those under a curse will fail at everything they try to do:

- They will experience chronic or life threatening diseases such as diabetes and cancer.
- Mental illnesses including suicide will haunt them.
- They will suffer marital conflict.
- Their children will be in bondage.
- They will be in continued financial lack.

If your life manifests any of these effects, you might be under a curse, but only the Holy Spirit can make the proper diagnosis. It is likely to be a "generational" curse if your parents also experienced the same thing - or something similar. If so, it is time to address the issue of demons.

THE NEED FOR REPARATIONS

In order to break the curse you must understand whether it originated with you or with your parents, grandparents, or great grandparents. If it began with them, then you need to confess the sins of your relatives.

"What?" you may ask. It is scriptural to confess the sins of the previous generation. Look at an example in Nehemiah's life: *Then I said: "O Lord, God of heaven, the great and awesome God, who keeps his covenant of love with those who love him and obey his commands, let your ear be attentive and your eyes open to hear the prayer your servant is praying before you day and night for your servants, the people of Israel. I confess the sins we Israelites, including myself and my father's house, have committed against you"* (Nehemiah 1:5-6).

Nehemiah confessed not only *his* sins but also the transgressions of his *father's house.* He went back to the past to make things right.

Some might wonder why this is necessary. I believe that if we ignore the past we are liable to repeat it. If we do not become totally honest regarding the sins of our forefathers, we may fall into them ourselves.

> ***If we do not become totally honest regarding the sins of our forefathers, we may fall into them ourselves.***

Secrecy and Denial

Research has shown that the reason it is hard for children to break free from the patterns set by their parents is because they try to keep secret their parents' lifestyle – or they simply deny their behavior. Secrecy and denial are the culprits of perpetuating the generational curse.

The Bible says to establish everything by two or three witnesses and I want to give you another scripture that enforces the need to confess the sins of our fathers: *O Lord, we acknowledge our wickedness and the guilt of our fathers; we have indeed sinned against you* (Jeremiah 14:20).

There is the evidence: two scriptural witnesses that stress the need to confess *our fathers' guilt* when we have followed in their footsteps.

Let me take this further. Not only must we confess and repent from our father's sin, we must also, if possible, make reparations for our fathers.

"Now wait a minute, Pastor Brown!" I can hear some complain. "How can I do that?"

Here is what I mean. Let's say, for example, your father was a racist. Then you need to work now at race reconciliation. It is not enough that you abstain from making racist remarks, you need to take action to help bring about harmony. Do the exact opposite that your father did. That is true repentance.

IT HAPPENED TO ME

In my case, my father was abusive to my mother. He was a bar owner, and drank heavily. He rarely spent time with me and my sister, and never took us on a vacation.

When I was a baby, my mother, also, was not a good example of motherhood. Wanting to continue her party lifestyle, she gave us up to my grandmother. In addition, my grandmother and grandfather were not kind to each other while we lived with them. They even lived in separate bedrooms.

As you probably gathered, I was under a generational curse. This is why I feel so strongly about breaking such cycles.

Without the Lord, I would have continued in the pattern set by my parents.

WHERE DOES IT END?

I can see that without the Lord I would have continued in the pattern set by my parents. Thankfully, I came to Christ and understood clearly that this lifestyle must end with me. Otherwise, my children would be doomed to repeat history.

I made a conscious effort not only to repent for my father and mother's sins, I made a strong stand against their disappointing behavior.

For example, when a wife tells me that her husband has been abusive to her, I counsel the wife that she is permitted to leave her husband based on scripture. *"I hate divorce," says the Lord God of Israel, "and I hate a man covering his wife with violence as well..."* (Malachi 2:16).

The Lord is disgusted with both divorce and domestic violence. A husband cannot expect the wife to stay in the marriage if he beats her. When a husband abuses his wife it is equal to divorce. Therefore, I do not feel that a woman is constrained to stay in such a relationship. Of course, I am not advocating easy divorce, but no wife should feel any religious obligation to stay in the marriage.

When I counsel abusive men in my office, I am extremely stern with them. Why? I believe it is my duty to reverse the damage my father had done.

I do the same thing with drunkenness. I saw my dad inebriated every night as he staggered home from the bar. I have made sure that my children will never be able to say that they saw their father intoxicated, even once!

WHAT A CHANGE!

To counter what happened in my childhood, I have taken my family on vacations as often as I can, usually two or three times a year.

As demanding as child rearing may be, I have tried to give my children time – the very thing I did not experience growing up. I have been far from perfect, but I know the importance of making a diligent effort to truly abandon the sins of the past generation. I believe God has honored my effort. I have experienced the blessing of God instead of the curse.

What about my parents now? I can happily say that my dad gave his heart to the Lord, and I was privileged to baptize him in water. He was one of the first members of our church, and rarely did he miss a service while he was healthy.

Whatever happened in the past can end in your life.

My mother was saved before me and brought me to a knowledge of the Lord. She is now a very devoted wife, mother and grandmother. She spends more time with her children and grandchildren than the average mother and grandmother.

What a complete turn-around! She has become a tremendous blessing and a great example. The generational curse has ended in our lives.

SWEEP THE PAST CLEAN

Whatever happened in the past can *end* in your life. Confess your family's sins right now: Say, "In the name of Jesus, I confess my sins and my ancestor's sins. [You may want to be specific.] I refuse to allow the past to determine my future. I renounce and reject all past sins. I will work to make things right to the best of my ability."

The next thing you need to do is get rid of any idolatrous objects that may have been passed onto you, such as statutes, beads, relics, crystals, lucky charms and paintings that were used in idolatry.

You do not need to get rid of the gifts from your parents or grandparents that are not associated with what scripture calls "idols."

You may also need to destroy or return to the original

owners any *blood money* - money from gambling, stolen objects, etc.

The Cleansing Blood

After cleaning your house of these objects, claim your future in Christ. Although you may have inherited bad blood, the blood of Jesus will cleanse you from *all* sin. You need to believe more in the power of His precious blood than the power of your ancestors' blood.

Then release yourself from the curse through prayer. Words are vital. A curse is by definition words spoken against someone. So to free yourself from the curse you must *speak* over yourself. You must declare God's blessings on your life.

To accomplish this objective, you may want to use this prayer:

> *In the name of Jesus, I declare that I am a child of God. The blood of Jesus has regenerated me. I do not have to live under any curse. Christ has redeemed me from the curse of the Law. I take my authority as a child of God and I release my grandchildren, my children and myself from the generational curse. I command every demon to leave my bloodline, right now! By Jesus' stripes we are healed and blessed!*

Since the prayer of faith is powerful and effective, you must not doubt. If you pray in uncertainty or fear, your prayers will be cancelled. *Believe* that the demons have left you and your family.

"I THANK YOU!"

Stand in faith. Instead of repeating this prayer over and over again, offer a prayer of thanksgiving.

Say *"I thank you, Father, that I am free from the generational curse. I do not inherit anything from my parents or grandparents. I am a new creation in Christ Jesus. Old things are passed away and all things are new. I live under the new covenant with better blessings. I am blessed in the city and blessed in the country. Everything I set my hands to do is blessed. My children are blessed too. I am the head and not the tail, above only and not beneath."*

Claim your deliverance!

PART II

MENTAL DISEASES

CHAPTER 4

HEALING FOR THE WHOLE MAN

There is a marvelous story in John's gospel about Jesus going to Jerusalem for a feast of the Jews.

Now there is in Jerusalem near the Sheep Gate a pool, which in Aramaic is called Bethesda and which is surrounded by five covered colonnades. Here a great number of disabled people used to lie – the blind, the lame, the paralyzed. One who was there had been an invalid for thirty-eight years. When Jesus saw him lying there and learned that he had been in this condition for a long time, he asked him, "Do you want to get well?"

"Sir," the invalid replied, "I have no one to help me into the pool when the water is stirred. While I am trying to get in, someone else goes down ahead of me." Then Jesus said to him, "Get up! Pick up your mat and walk." At once the man was cured; he picked up his mat and walked. The day on which this took place was a Sabbath...Later Jesus found him at the temple and said to him, "See, you are well again. Stop sinning or something worse may happen to you" (John 5:1-9, 14).

What was Jesus' commentary on this man's healing? He

said to them, *"I did one miracle, and you are all astonished. Yet, because Moses gave you circumcision (though actually it did not come from Moses, but from the patriarchs), you circumcise a child on the Sabbath. Now if a child can be circumcised on the Sabbath so that the law of Moses may not be broken, why are you angry with me for healing the whole man on the Sabbath?"* (John 7:21-23).

The phrase that made an impact on me is *why are you angry with me for healing the whole man...?* Jesus healed not just "part" of the individual but the total, complete man.

"STOP SINNING!"

There were greater problems with this individual than met the eye. At first glance, it seemed as though all that was needed was physical healing, however, a closer examination reveals far more. Jesus told him, *"Stop sinning or something worse may happen to you."*

It was a sin problem as well as a physical problem.

Most people who attend a miracle crusade are looking for physical healing, but they also need a spiritual touch. They need to be healed from sin.

In addition, this man had an *attitude* problem. Jesus asked him if he wanted to be healed, and the man, feeling sorry for himself, said, "I have no one to help me!"

I'm certain you have met people who need an attitude adjustment. The man at the pool of Bethesda complained, "While I am trying to get in, someone else goes down ahead of me."

Do you know people like that? It is always someone else's fault, never their own. Perhaps you have the same problem. Let me assure you that Jesus can also heal *your* attitude.

The point of this story is simple: Christ has come to heal the "whole" person. He wants to perform a *complete* miracle – not just a partial one.

This is what deliverance healing can accomplish – healing of our spirit, soul and body.

WHAT IS MAN?

He wants to perform a complete miracle – not just a partial one.

How do we know that man is comprised of these three elements (spirit, soul and body)? The Bible tells us so. God's Word is the scalpel that dissects mankind for us so that we might know what we are comprised of.

Every medical student is required to dissect a cadaver. This is an essential part of their training because they need to be acquainted with every part of the human body.

Since Jesus came to heal the whole person, it is important to understand the totality of man. There is more to us than meets the eye. Even the Psalmist writes, "What is man?"

This ancient question must be answered. The only one who truly knows us is God. Since He is the Creator, He understands the complexity of His creation.

If I own a Toyota, I do not take it to a Ford dealership for repairs. I take it to the manufacturer. Likewise, if you are sick, you call on the One who created you – and the manufacturer is God.

After years of medical education, doctors still do not fully understand the intricacies of man. In the last century we saw the birth of a new science called psychiatry. This branch of medicine was born from the medical world's realization that our mind can affect our health.

The more science studies the human species, the more it realizes how unique we really are. So who is man? The answer must come from God, since He is the one who made us.

SPIRIT, SOUL AND BODY

Here is what the Bible says: *May God himself, the God of peace, sanctify you through and through. May your whole spirit, soul and body be kept blameless at the coming of our Lord Jesus Christ* (1Thessalonians 5:23).

The Lord does not want you only healed, He wants you complete, not lacking anything!

You need *total* blessing – not just part of you; all of you. As Paul exclaims, *"May your whole spirit, soul and body."* He uses the word *whole.*

A favorite phrase spoken by Jesus when healing the sick was "Be whole!" The Lord does not want you only *healed*, He wants you complete, not lacking anything!

It was the custom of the writers in Paul's day to list things in order of priority. When the apostle said, "spirit, soul and body," it is clear that the spirit is the most important part of us. It is the God-side of us.

- Our spirit make us like the Father.
- Our spirit desires to fellowship with the Creator.
- Our spirit draws us to believe in God's existence.

As hard as atheists may try, I believe they can't shake off their unconscious awareness of God's existence.

Paul also mentions the soul and body. There you have all three parts of man mentioned in the New Testament. Paul, however, received this revelation of man's three-part nature through the Old Testament, primarily through the two creation accounts.

DUST AND BREATH

The first chronicle of creation (Genesis chapter 1) emphasizes the *nobility* of man, and the second account (Genesis chapter 2) reveals the *humility* of man.

The first account reveals three things about man:

1. He is made in God's image.
2. He has dominion over the animals.
3. He enjoys a different food source than the animals.

God said, *"Let us make man in our image, in our likeness, and let them rule over the fish of the sea and the birds of the air, over the livestock, over all the earth, and over all the creatures that move along the ground." So God created man in his own image, in the image of God he created him; male and female he created them* (Genesis 1:26-27).

I am awestruck each time I read this! We are made in God's image. The Creator Himself was the pattern for man.

He then reminds us that we should rule the animals: *God blessed them and said to them, "Be fruitful and increase in number; fill the earth and subdue it. Rule over the fish of the sea and the birds of the air and over every living creature that moves on the ground"* (Genesis 1:28).

OUR SUPREMACY

God tells us that we are in charge of creation – which means we must also take care of it, including the animals. If you stop to think about it, we are the only species that cares about preserving *all* creatures.

To show man's supremacy and nobility over the rest of creation God gives mankind a different food source. *Then God said, "I give you every seed-bearing plant on the face of the whole earth and every tree that has fruit with seed in it. They will be yours for food. And to all the beasts of the earth and all the birds of the air and all the creatures that move on the ground-everything that has the breath of life in it – I give every green plant for food." And it was so* (Genesis 1:29-30).

Animals are given plants for food, but for mankind, we receive *every seed-bearing plant* and *fruit with seed in it.* How does this relate to man's supremacy? Animals cannot appreciate the laws of sowing and reaping. God reminds man that he knows about this divine law. Even Jesus remarked, *Look at the birds of the air; they do not sow or reap or store away in barns, and yet your heavenly Father feeds them. Are you not much more valuable than they?* (Matthew 6:26).

We have greater worth than animals because we know about seedtime and harvest.

We have greater worth than animals because we know about seedtime and harvest.

A HUMBLING TRUTH

And the Lord God formed man of the dust of the ground, and breathed into his nostrils the breath of life; and man became a living soul (Genesis 2:7 KJV).

This second account of creation reveals both noble and humble things about man:

1. Man is formed from dust.
2. Man has a spirit that comes from God.
3. Man is an eternal soul.

Let's look at the first fact. The passage says that God made man from the *dust of the ground.*

At first glance, we do not seem that much different from the animals. Scientists have discovered that what separates a gorilla from a human is only one chromosome. Think about it! That is rather humbling. Compare us to rodents, and the similarity is still there. Our genes are only fractions apart.

How could this be? It is because animals also came from the same source as man: *Now the Lord God had formed out of the ground all the beasts of the field and all the birds of the air. He brought them to the man to see what he would name them; and whatever the man called each living creature, that was its name (Genesis 2:19).*

HIGHER AUTHORITY

God brought into being *all* the animals from the ground - man, beasts and birds. So mankind is similar in certain respects to the animals. This is why scientists can experiment with rats to find medical cures for human diseases.

The passage also reveals man's higher nobility. He was given the right to name the animals. This reflects man's authority; much like a parent who names their child or the business person who names the company. Man is in charge of all creatures, yet the scripture also reveals that he comes from the dust of the ground.

Looking closely at the previous verse we see three important aspects of man's origin:

1. Man's *body* was formed from the dust of the ground. Physically we are like animals.
2. God breathed into man the breath of life. Breath speaks of *spirit*.
3. The result of the union of spirit and body was the soul. Man became a living *soul*.

THE BREATH OF LIFE

The Creator took His own substance, His own essence, and transferred it to man.

We have discussed the making of our body, but what about our spirit?

Hebrew and Greek words for spirit can also be translated breath or wind. Since Jesus called God a spirit (John 4:24) we know that the Father took something of Himself and placed it into man. In simple language, *God breathed into man the breath of life.*

The Creator took His own substance, His own essence, and transferred it to us. As a result, we have a spirit made in the likeness of God. However, notice carefully that the Almighty breathed into man's *nostrils* the breath of life. He did not breathe into his mouth. This was not mouth to mouth resuscitation. He did mouth to nostrils! (Genesis 2:7).

If you can imagine the picture: God is breathing into

man's nostrils, which elevates Him above man. The Lord reminds man that no matter how closely he is to being like God he still is beneath the Father. The Psalmist exclaims, *For thou hast made him but little lower than God, And crownest him with glory and honor*" (Psalm 8:5 ASV).

Man is lifted up, yet he still remains subservient to God.

WHAT MAKES US HUMAN?

Where does the soul fit into the picture? The result of the union of spirit and body was that *man became a living soul.* He did not *receive* a soul, nor was one created for him. No! Man *became* a soul. It is what we are!

We are not bodies and spirits, we are souls – and that makes us human. It is what separates us from animals and even from being like God.

The message is clear: our bodies relate to animals, our spirits relate to God, and our souls relate to the human race. To put it another way: our bodies make us like animals, our spirits make us like God, and our souls make us like humans.

When the Lord provided healing, He did it for the *whole* man!

Chapter 5

What Is the Soul?

The words, "*and man became a living soul* (Genesis 2:7 KJV), describe our present condition – what we *became*.

Certainly we would love to be a living *spirit*. From the beginning it was man's wish to be like God. That desire, however, as noble as it seems, became the cause of man's failure. The serpent slithered to Eve and said, *For God knows that when you eat of it your eyes will be opened, and you will be like God, knowing good and evil* (Genesis 3:5).

Adam and Eve were tired of being so human; they wanted to be like God. This was their chance to become totally divine. No longer would they remain lower than God; they would be equal to Him. They were wrong!

This is the same dilemma mankind faces today. Are we willing to allow the Creator to rule our souls, or do we want our souls to rule our lives? There is a familiar song that says, "I am the captain of my soul!" Once you become the master of your soul, then you will soon discover how unqualified you really are to guide the affairs of your life.

THE BREATH OF GOD

Since we are a living soul, we need to understand what that truly encompasses. The Hebrew word for soul is *nephesh*. It means to breathe, and is related to the breath of God.

We must recognize that God is spirit - He breathed, man inhaled, and so was born the soul. In other words, the spirit is the breath *out*; the soul is the breath *in*.

The soul is the *breathing* we do because of God's breath. However, it only shows how related the soul is to the spirit - you cannot have one without the other.

When it comes to defining the soul, the New Testament is a great help. It was written in Greek and the word it uses for soul is *psuche* (pronounced, psoo-khay'). It also means breath, and carries an additional meaning of the rational and immortal side to us. Thus, soul means the mind. It is where the word "psyche" comes from.

The biblical proverb says, *"For as he thinketh in his heart, so is he"* (Proverbs 23:7 KJV).

You are the sum total of your thoughts.

WHO ARE YOU?

When you think about who you really are, you must conclude that you are the sum total of your thoughts. Let me illustrate what I mean.

Suppose your arm was amputated, and my arm replaced it. Have you now become me? Hardly. You continue to be yourself with Tom Brown's arm. Then imagine you lose *both* your arms and mine replaces them, have you changed being you? Of course not, you continue to be yourself.

Let's proceed. You lose your legs and receive mine instead, are you still you? Yes, of course. Suppose my eyes replace yours, have you changed from being you? No. Regardless of how many parts of my body you receive as replacements, they do not change your personality.

However, what if you keep all your limbs, and only my *mind* replaces yours? You look the same; your vocal chords remain, but your body has undergone a fundamental change of personality. If my mind was in your body, then my personality has transferred to your body. Though I may look like you, I am really me! Why? My mind is who I am. I am my soul.

The Bible says, "Man became a living soul." That is who I am – soul and mind. Therefore, the real me can be found in my thoughts!

THE BUTTERFLY

The true change God desires to make in us is with our minds. In Greek the word *psyche* is also the name for butterfly. A caterpillar undergoes metamorphosis and becomes a butterfly. Paul uses this analogy to speak of being *"transformed by the renewing of your mind"* (Romans 12:2).

The word *transformed* is the Greek word *metamorphoo*, which is where we get our word "metamorphose." There is no greater transformation in nature than a caterpillar becoming a butterfly.

If God had not breathed into man, then we would be no different than the animals. However, man *is* different because he was transformed into a soul.

Giraffes are known for their necks, whales for their size, cheetahs for their speed, while mankind's predominant feature is his mind. Let's face it, man's intellect is far superior to the animals. This is what Genesis 2 states. Man became a living soul, a living mind.

The seat of the soul – the mind – comprises the emotions, intellect and reasoning ability. It is our greatest asset, and also the source of our greatest problems.

THE STORY OF PSYCHE

In classical Greek, Psyche was the personification of the soul of a beautiful girl who was loved by Eros.

According to the most romantic of the Greek and Roman myths, the lovely Psyche had, through her great beauty, incited jealousy in the heart of Venus, the goddess of love. The son of Venus, Eros, was told by his jealous mother to inspire Psyche with the love of some other creature. Yet when he arrived, he fell in love with her. It is the soul that makes us beautiful.

Every night he would come to Psyche and tell her that she must not ask for his name or gaze upon him. Then one night, after being prodded by her two sisters, she lit a lamp and saw Eros. She too fell in love, but when the oil from the lamp fell upon Eros he was awakened and quickly vanished.

In her despair, Psyche went to Venus to beg forgiveness and offer to do deeds of penance. Venus was unforgiving and assigned the most difficult of tasks to the beautiful girl, but Eros rescued her and at his appeal she was received among the gods who united the lovers in marriage.

You might see a resemblance of the biblical story, even though the characters are different. The Bible – a real story, not a myth – tells of God's love for us, and the penalties for our failure to submit to His authority. Consequently, just like Psyche, our souls are overworked with tasks that we can hardly bear.

Notice the relationship between the two curses placed on Adam and Eve. Adam would *toil* for his food. Eve would *labor* to give birth to children. The similarity is obvious: they both would work. That is the burden of the soul. It must work! And this is a curse not a blessing.

REST FOR YOUR SOULS

Look around and you will see many afflicted people - sick not only in their bodies, but in their souls. Why are they sick? It is because they are restless, not wanting Christ to guide their inner man. Like Eros, Jesus wants to rescue us from our burdens: *Come to me, all you who are weary and burdened, and I will give you rest. Take my yoke upon you and learn from me, for I am gentle and humble in heart, and you will find rest for your souls. For my yoke is easy and my burden is light* (Matthew 11:28-30).

Look around and you will see many afflicted people – sick not only in in their bodies, but in their souls.

The word "disease" is based on two words: *dis* meaning "not" and *ease* meaning "rest." Disease literally means "not at ease" or not at rest. That is the *real* disease.

Our society is in constant turmoil. Americans pride themselves on being strong, yet Americans – who represent only six percent of the world's population - consume ninety percent of the world's tranquilizers. The rest of the nations do not fare much better.

A recent study listed the ten leading causes of disabilities worldwide (measured in years lived with a disability). Five were psychiatric conditions: depression, alcohol use, manic depression, schizophrenia and obsessive-compulsive disorders. Such conditions account for almost eleven percent of the disease burden worldwide. Almost two million Americans suffer from manic depression.

Daytime talk shows reveal a society that is deeply troubled. People screaming obscenities, throwing chairs, trading punches and pulling hair. Is this what we have become? And the public wants to see more! Perhaps they feel better if they see people more troubled than themselves.

It has become abundantly clear that mankind is not emotionally healthy.

An unknown author penned a verse describing the problem. It could be our national anthem:

We mutter and sputter, we fume and we spurt;
We mumble and grumble, our feelings get hurt;
We can't understand things, our vision grows dim,
When all that we need is communion with Him!

More than the Mind

In this life, our thoughts are contained within the brain. However, the soul is not the brain – the organ of thought.

Beyond this earthly existence, our thoughts continue. Why is this true? Because, in reality, the soul is that invisible, immortal part of you that makes up your personality and it affects your mind and emotions.

Here is what Jesus said about the soul: *Do not be afraid of those who kill the body but cannot kill the soul* (Matthew 10:28).

Although the brain may die, our soul continues beyond

the grave. It cannot die. *What good is it for a man to gain the whole world, yet forfeit his soul?* (Mark 8:36). Or, as Luke wrote, *What good is it for a man to gain the whole world, and yet lose or forfeit his very self?* (Luke 9:25).

Luke translates Marks version of the soul as being *his very self.* The soul is more than the mind; it is the real you that determines what you think. Why do you feel restless? It is because of wrong thoughts.

The soul is more than the mind; it is the real you that determines what you think.

SOUL-DESTROYING DEMONS

A demon does not appear simply to make your body sick. Why should it bother with something as insignificant as flesh and bone, when the soul is far more enticing?

When people come to our crusades for healing, they often limit miracles as applying only to the body, but as I minister they quickly learn they need healing for the soul.

The scriptures are quick to point out that Satan and his demons attack the mind. *But I am afraid that just as Eve was deceived by the serpent's cunning, your minds may somehow be led astray from your sincere and pure devotion to Christ.* (2 Corinthians 11:3).

It is clear that Satan will try to steer you away from the right path by leading *your minds* astray – that is where demons primarily work. If the devil has control over your mind, then he has you!

Consider Paul's statement concerning spiritual warfare: *For though we live in the world, we do not wage war as the world does. The weapons we fight with are not the weapons of the world. On the contrary, they have divine power to demolish strongholds. We demolish arguments and every pretension that sets itself up against the knowledge of God, and we take captive every thought to make it obedient to Christ* (2 Corinthians 10:3-5).

Arguments and thoughts are part of the mind. That is where the battle is being waged. It is also why we must *demolish arguments* and *take captive every thought.*

Emotional Attacks

What is the easiest part of the soul to attack? Our emotions.

When someone is being assaulted by demons, it is usually their emotions that are first to buckle under the strain. People suffer nervous breakdowns, or at the very least, experience panic attacks.

If you suffer such attacks, the anxiety may cause you to feel dizzy or nauseated. It is more than just feeling sick. You have the sensation that reality is slipping away from you, and you may even feel you're about to die, or are going to lose your mind. Your heart is pounding – and you can't catch your breath. You break out in a cold sweat, wanting to escape.

Panic attacks cripple your activity. How? Because, when you anticipate anxiety, you avoid any situations in which you have had previous attacks. Therefore, you may refuse to go out alone or may develop any number of terrifying phobias.

Is this your experience? These onslaughts are from Satan. He is controlling your mind. Thankfully, you can overcome him through the Word of God.

"THIS IS MY ANSWER!"

My stepfather, Red, suffered terrible panic attacks. He felt that he was going crazy and wanted freedom, but did not know where to turn for answers.

Then one Sunday morning I was teaching on the power of the spoken Word of God. I explained that Jesus used only one weapon against Satan – He spoke the written scriptures out loud to the devil. When Jesus did, Satan fled. I then gave our congregation a list of several scriptures to speak out loud every day of their lives.

The thought hit Red, *This is my answer. I am going to speak the Word of God!*

"I am going to speak the Word of God!"

When the next panic attack came, he opened his mouth and began to quote the scriptures. As he describes the feeling: "I could feel the black cloud over me suddenly vanish when I began to confess the Word of God."

He is very eager to tell his story to whoever is facing a similar problem. The Word works!

Maybe you do not suffer from anxiety disorders, but nevertheless you are far from being at peace! How can you tell when this is your condition? The psalmist describes a soul that is not at rest: He said, *"Oh, that I had wings of a dove! I would fly away and be at rest"* (Psalm 55:6).

Emotions are a part of the soul. The Latin word for emotions is *ex-mover*, which means to move away.

If you feel you want to escape – to leave your city, your job, or even worse, your family – recognize that your soul is being attacked by demons.

Thank God, there is an answer!

CHAPTER 6

THE SPIRIT OF FEAR

You do not have to wonder about the source of fear. The Bible says, *For God hath not given us the spirit of fear; but of power, and of love, and of a sound mind* (2 Timothy 1:7 KJV).

This scripture is blunt. Fear is called a *spirit.* Another New Testament verse confirms that it is a demon: *For you did not receive a spirit that makes you a slave again to fear* (Romans 8:15).

Fear is not just an emotion, it is a spirit that *enslaves* you. Sure, it produces feelings and affects us deeply, yet there is more to fear than an emotional distress. It is a spiritual force.

I am sometimes asked by reporters how I can tell whether a person's emotional problems are demons or simply psychological. The truth is the Bible teaches that the root of many problems are demons, yet the fruit may be emotional symptoms. You may see a fruit on the tree, however, the life force of the fruit is hidden underground. You can't see the roots, yet they are there.

The fruit can be seen through symptoms – fear, depression, anxiety – while the root is the invisible operation of demons. A psychologist can rightly diagnose someone as having a certain phobia, yet the diagnosis falls short of explaining the source of the problem. The Bible explains that fears come from the kingdom of darkness.

People find relief when they discover the origin of their anxiety. It is much easier to deal with the specific spirits producing the fear than to try to deal with some abstract cause. Fear is produced by demons that speak words into your mind.

Fear is produced by demons that speak words into your mind.

As we have seen in the previous chapter, you must *take captive every thought.* Concepts and ideas may try to run wild, but you must imprison and confine them to the judgment of God.

GOOD FEAR?

Granted, there are some fears that are normal and not demonic. In certain cases, they can actually be *good.* For example, the Bibles tells us to fear the Lord.

Another word for fear is caution. *Eulabeia* is the Greek word for the fear of doing something that can be harmful or dangerous to your life, both physically and spiritually. It is a mechanism to help us deal with danger and keep us from acting like daredevils.

This kind of fear is short lived. We face it during a moment of crisis. For example, my son, Justin, developed a swollen eye and we were obviously concerned about him. That worry turned into positive action on our part. We took him to the doctor and discovered that he had a rare infection, which, if left untreated, could have resulted in the loss of his eye. The doctor prescribed medicine for him and told us to keep a good eye on him (no pun intended). If the swelling did not go down within two days, he told us to rush him to the hospital.

After twenty-four hours, I noticed no improvement. I felt led of the Lord to look at the expiration date on the medicine bottle and found that it expired that day. So I made the pharmacy exchange the medicine. Within hours the swelling subsided.

This kind of fear is actually good. It helps protect our loved ones and us from danger and harm. Some prefer to call it *concern* instead of fear, but whatever you name it, do not confuse this with bad fear.

THRIVING IN DIFFICULTY

I remember hearing the story of a woman who lifted an automobile to save her child. She was driving her car when she became involved in an accident. The car flipped on its side, right on her child, who was trapped underneath.

Without thinking, the woman jumped out of the vehicle, lifted it up and pulled her child from the wreckage to safety.

What gave her that strength? It was the fear that her child would die.

This kind of fright gives us a boost of adrenaline in order to protect others and ourselves. It is available when needed to help us overcome obstacles and perform to the best of our abilities.

I think of Joe Montana, arguably the best quarterback to ever play football. He thrived in difficult situations. The more hopeless the circumstances, the better he played. This is an example of a *good* kind of fear that we call on when we need to be victorious.

TORMENTING FEAR

For some people, it seems the anxiety never ends. The mother who pulled her child from the car wreck, may be afraid to drive or she could become overprotective. Now we are dealing with an unhealthy fear. It is what John talks about when he writes, *Fear hath torment* (1 John 4:18 KJV). The Greek word is *phobos* – fear that has turned negative. This type of concern no longer enables you to overcome or increase your performance. It is tormenting, even demonic.

A severe anxiety of this nature hinders the believer from enjoying life and freezes people from doing the will of God. It may be the dread of flying – perhaps you need to travel overseas to preach, but boarding a plane paralyzes you and you just can't go.

You long to visit your out of town relatives, yet they live thousands of miles away, so you stay home, fearful to fly. It is illogical thinking. You know that flying is safer than driving, yet you don't care. Your anxiety has made you irrational.

There are all kinds of phobias that hinder people from enjoying the abundant life that Jesus came to give. It could be something harmless – like swimming. You may never need to swim, but does it keep you from boarding a ship? If it does, then it is hurting your freedom.

Are you afraid of crowds? If so, does it keep you from going to church? If that is the case, it is probably demonic and you need to overcome it through Christ.

INSTANT DELIVERANCE

I know a man who was afraid to hold hands with others while praying. He felt that his hands would curse people. It was irrational and he knew it. He was delivered by the power of God and is now a mighty prayer warrior.

The psalmist found the solution: *I sought the Lord, and he answered me; he delivered me from all my fears* (Psalm 34:4).

One of the greatest aspects of deliverance is that it is *instant*. People rarely overcome fears gradually. If they try to improve slowly, they often find themselves in a worse condition than before. God will deliver you *now* from the spirits that have placed you in bondage.

I remember how my youngest son, Caleb, was deathly afraid of fireworks. He would bury his head in his lap, close his ears, and try to shut out the noise. One day, on the fourth of July, we were awaiting the firework display at the end of a baseball game. Caleb was about to follow the routine of burying his head when I stopped him.

> ***"Caleb," I told him, "you do not need to be afraid of fireworks."***

"Caleb," I told him, "you do not need to be afraid of fireworks. The Lord is about to deliver you from this fear."

He looked at me and said, "Really?"

"Absolutely!" I said. Then I took my hands and placed them on his head and I drove out the spirit of fear. When I did, I told him, "The spirit of fear has left you. You can now enjoy the fireworks."

He smiled and when the show began, not batting an eye,

he looked up into the sky and enjoyed every blast. Then Caleb turned to me and smiled, "Dad, I'm not afraid anymore."

I believe in instant deliverance from fear. You can experience it immediately.

NOT FEAR, BUT POWER

There are three forces that help us overcome. We find them in these words the apostle Paul wrote to young Timothy.

For God hath not given us the spirit of fear; but of power, and of love, and of a sound mind (2 Timothy 1:7 KJV).

Why are we fearful? Because we feel powerless and helpless to change a situation. When we have authority to get rid of something evil, then fear cannot take command.

The Bible says that we have power to resist the devil, and he will flee from us. We can heal the sick. We can call on angels for protection. We *do* have power, and can overcome evil with good.

When you recognize that you are in control, then fear must leave. It cannot coexist with power.

When you recognize that you are in control, then fear must leave. It cannot coexist with power.

NOT FEAR, BUT LOVE

The Bible also shows the correlation between love and fear. As John wrote, *There is no fear in love. But perfect love drives out fear, because fear has to do with punishment. The one who fears is not made perfect in love* (1 John 4:18).

Just as fear cannot coexist with power, it cannot live together with love. You have either one or the other.

In the above passage, John shows that the person who is fearful doubts God's love for him. When you know that God loves you, then you also know He will help and not hurt you.

We are often afraid because we believe we deserve punishment – thinking God is out to chastise us. It's just the opposite; our Father longs to help us.

I have heard sermons that give the impression God causes trouble in the lives of believers. I don't understand how people can read the Word and conclude that the Lord punishes those who obey Him.

I can't speak for you, but I know God loves me. I don't live with the constant dread that the Almighty will harm me – since the punishment for my sins has already occurred at the cross. God loved me so much that He sent His son, Jesus, who took my place. He atoned for my sin, so that I would never have to face eternal punishment.

I totally rely on God's love for me.

NOT FEAR, BUT A SOUND MIND

Fear attacks our thought process. This is why Paul says we are not to have a spirit of fear, but a *sound mind.*

God did not create your thinking to handle worry and anxiety. Your mind is not wired for fear any more than it's wired for electricity. Stick a fork in an electric outlet, and you'll be in for a shock!

I read the story about an underclassman, who went through an initiation for his fraternity. They blindfolded him and tied him to the railroad tracks. What he was unaware of was that there were another set of tracks close by. All he heard was the deafening sound of the oncoming train. As it approached closer and closer he screamed for help. His fraternity brothers just laughed. Finally after the train passed by, the young men went to untie their friend, but they found him dead. He died of a heart attack!

Jesus spoke of *Men's hearts failing them for fear* (Luke 21:26).

You may not die as this freshman did, but you may experience another kind of death. It happens when you begin to lose courage. Without it you will never be able to win life's battles.

DEMONS ARE AFRAID!

What is the number one weapon of a terrorist? *Fear!*

Isaiah prophesied concerning what it could do. *Whoever flees at the sound of terror will fall into a pit* (Isaiah 24:18). That is the goal of those who would try to destroy us.

The reason terrorists use this weapon is because they are acquainted firsthand with fear. In fact, they are themselves afraid – worried they may lose their way of life. They see America as bigger and stronger, and they dread losing power. They also worry that Christianity will dwarf their religion. So they bomb our buildings in order to make us cower and run. However, the truth is, they are more frightened of us than we are of them.

It's the same with demons. They are called "spirits of fear" because that is what they are. The reason a particular spirit produces panic in you is because the spirits are afraid. Their presence brings anxiety and consternation – and fear breeds fear.

According to scripture, *You believe that there is one God. Good! Even the demons believe that - and shudder* (James 2:19).

ROARING LIONS

Demons quake in God's presence. Since the Lord lives in you, they *should* tremble in fear when you know who you are in Christ. *Be self-controlled and alert. Your enemy the devil prowls around like a roaring lion looking for someone to devour* (1 Peter 5:8).

Demons quake in God's presence.

Lions do not roar when they are ready to attack their prey - only when they feel threatened. Like the devil, they roar to scare and intimidate you.

I have never met a lion, but I have encountered a Doberman Pinscher. I was riding my bicycle when the menacing dog ran into the street. He was about 30 meters away when I quickly jumped off my bike. My heart was pounding, and my initial reaction was to get back on the bike and peddle away as fast as I could. But I knew he would catch me, so I ran *toward* him screaming, "Ahhhhh!" The dog stopped dead in his tracks, turned away and fled.

The animal was more afraid of me than I was of him! This is what James meant went he wrote: *Resist the devil, and he will flee from you* (James 4:7).

The word *flee* means to run in stark terror. Satan is afraid, but does not want to let you know it. When you feel threatened, know for certain that demons have more fear of you than you have of them.

"I Am Not Afraid!"

It is time that you purpose to live fear-free. When you feel engulfed with great anxiety, attack it by quoting scripture.

Here is a confession of the Word of God that you can use:

> *I fear not, for God has not given me the spirit of fear but He has given me power, love and a sound mind. I have a peaceful, quiet mind – the mind of Christ.*
>
> *I am not afraid because God will provide for my children and my needs.*
>
> *I am not afraid because I have more angels with me than there are demons with the enemy.*
>
> *I am not afraid because I am worth more than the sparrows.*
>
> *If God is for us, who can be against us! The Lord is on my side!*

CHAPTER 7

THE DEMON OF DEPRESSION

Depression is a modern medical term that was not used in biblical times. Instead, scripture presents other terminology to describe the same condition.

The Spirit of the Sovereign Lord is on me, because the Lord has anointed me to...provide for those who grieve in Zion-to bestow on them a crown of beauty instead of ashes, the oil of gladness instead of mourning, and a garment of praise instead of a spirit of despair (Isaiah 61:1-3).

The Bible calls depression the *spirit of despair* – in the King James Version it is the "spirit of heaviness." When people have this malady they often feel *heavy*, as if they were carrying the weight of the world on their shoulders.

After praying for people with depression, I hear them testify, "I feel light." That is their description of being released from this dreadful affliction.

Depression is a condition of the mind. As we have learned, Satan attacks our thoughts above everything else. It is no surprise then to find demons afflicting people with a spirit of gloom.

The Bible describes Saul as having a demon that depressed him. A current translation using modern terms describes Saul's condition: *But the Spirit of the Lord had left Saul, and instead, the Lord had sent a tormenting spirit that filled him with depression and fear.* (1 Samuel 16:14 Living).

Without getting into the theological ramifications of God sending an evil spirit, the important point is that Saul's condition was the result of a *tormenting spirit.*

Just as fear has torment, so does depression. I have been told that more people check into hospitals over this, than any other single reason. It is the leading cause of mental health problems. It is an epidemic!

IS IT REALLY A DEMON?

Some professionals may question whether depression is caused by demons or is it just a chemical imbalance. I don't pretend to be an expert in the field of psychiatry; I will leave that to others; but I hope psychiatrists don't pretend to be experts in theology.

I am happy with whatever medical specialists can do to help hurting people; at the same time, it is clear from my experience that prayer for deliverance has been extremely effective in relieving people from depression.

My focus is on the spiritual side of the issue. As one who believes in the infallibility of the Bible, I have concluded that demons are often involved in inducing a depressed state.

Saul has been a case study for many that are involved in the field of psychology. Some have diagnosed Saul with bipolar depression. They note that he had all the symptoms of the illness. Yet the Bible simply states that an evil spirit tormented him. Consider this: he would find relief when David played spiritual songs on his harp. It is clear that a heavenly focus helped Saul.

Here is one method of determining whether an evil spirit is involved with the depression: If the person feels better after focusing on the Lord, then it seems that the problem is spiritual and not simply medical. On the other hand, if the person does not improve after prayer or deliverance, then the individual may be suffering from purely a medical condition. I believe a minority of people fall into this category.

I have come to the conclusion that depression is almost always caused by something spiritual or mental.

I have come to the conclusion that depression is almost always caused by something spiritual or mental.

YOU ARE NOT ALONE

Paul wrote to the believers at Corinth, *For when we came into Macedonia, this body of ours had no rest, but we were harassed at every turn – conflicts on the outside, fears within. But God, who comforts the downcast, comforted us by the coming of Titus* (2 Corinthians 7:5-6).

What a joy to know that God consoles those whose spirits are low. The word for *comfort* is the Greek word *parakletos*. It means to come alongside someone.

The Lord is very close to those who are downcast. When someone experiences depression, God is there – waiting to help. This is just the opposite of the loneliness and isolation felt by those who do not know the Lord.

Depression is the call for God to arrive on the scene. So take heart if you are dispirited; you are not alone. The Father is near you and there are brighter days ahead.

DON'T REFUSE!

There is a passage that speaks clearly to this subject; it is also a warning: *A voice is heard in Ramah, weeping and great mourning, Rachel weeping for her children and refusing to be comforted, because they are no more* (Matthew 2:18).

It is possible to refuse to be comforted. You may feel so dejected that you are convinced there is no help. You tell yourself, "Nobody cares about me!"

Do you know what you are doing? By rejecting what is available you have become stubborn.

Let scripture uplift you! *Listen* to the Word and *do* what it says.

I like to use the word SAD as an acronym for the three causes of depression – Sin, Attitude, and Demons.

THE SIN QUESTION

The Lord said to Cain, *Why are you angry? Why is your face downcast? If you do what is right, will you not be accepted? But if you do not do what is right, sin is crouching at your door; it desires to have you, but you must master it* (Genesis 4:6-7).

This is the first case of depression recorded in the Bible, and the cause is obvious: Cain sinned by not offering God a better sacrifice. Consequently, the Lord refused to accept second best. Cain was upset when he saw his brother's gifts received by God. The Lord asked him a heart-probing question: "Why is your face downcast?" God wanted Cain to face the cause of his sorrow.

Sometimes we have an unexplained sadness. We can't determine its origin. However, if we are honest with ourselves, we may discover the reason for our depression is our sin. We have gone against our conscience and feel the guilt. The solution is that *we need to repent!*

Hours of therapy on a doctor's couch is not the answer. We must face the reality we have disobeyed the Lord and are suffering the consequences. Since sin depresses us, we dislike ourselves. We don't need deliverance from an evil spirit, we need repentance.

We don't need deliverance from an evil spirit. We need repentance.

DO WHAT IS RIGHT

A young college student was suicidal, because, according to him, his father was not giving him the approval he needed. The son told his counselor, "All my father does is complain about me."

"Does he act the same way toward your sister?"

"No," replied the young man, "she is his favorite."

The counselor wisely asked, "Is it true that she does well in school?"

"Yes, but what does that matter?"

"Well, I noticed that you are flunking two courses."

"So, what!" the student snapped, "My father has to accept me for who I am!"

The young man's problem was not his father. It was his failure to do what was right – and now he was angry and bitter.

You can't expect to be happy when you fail to do your best.

Don't be like Mark Twain, who stole a watermelon from a vendor and took it to the nearby river. He cut it open and after looking carefully at it, said, "This just isn't right? I don't feel right about eating this!"

So he went back to the store. When the salesman wasn't looking he put the watermelon back and took a *ripe* one instead!

Facing the Consequences

It is disappointing that many counselors have not acted as wisely as the one we have just mentioned. Instead of pointing out the need for people to improve their lives, they often side with the client - agreeing they are being mistreated. All this does is reinforce the negative behavior which continues the cycle of depression.

Things have changed among psychiatrists. They don't emphasize the need to listen to the conscience. For example, there was a time when the psychiatric field labeled homosexuality as a mental disorder. Now, through pressure from activists, they have altered their opinion and treat homosexuality as a healthy alternative. Despite the change in their diagnoses, there is still a high rate of suicide among homosexuals.

You can argue that they are mistreated, maligned and misunderstood, but their lifestyle remains the underlying problem. There needs to be repentance.

The same can be said about adultery. *Of course* people are upset after they are caught breaking their marriage vows. What do you expect? That is the consequence of sin. The answer to depression when it is sin-induced is to admit and confess our condition to God. It is the first step to deliverance.

THE ATTITUDE FACTOR

A death in the family, a divorce, a loss of income or deteriorating health can be devastating. Yet there is hope. The answer is your attitude – the way you perceive things. As the old analogy says, "Do you see a glass half *empty* or half *full*?"

As a Christian, our optimism is based on a faithful God, not on some utopian fantasy. We believe that all things will work out for our good. God has promised it! Our hope is based on His faithfulness.

David knew this kind of hope. He wrote, *As the deer pants for streams of water, so my soul pants for you, O God. My soul thirsts for God, for the living God. When can I go and meet with God? My tears have been my food day and night, while men say to me all day long, "Where is your God?" These things I remember as I pour out my soul: how I used to go with the multitude, leading the procession to the house of God, with shouts of joy and thanksgiving among the festive throng. Why are you downcast, O my soul? Why so disturbed within me? Put your hope in God, for I will yet praise him, my Savior and my God. My soul is downcast within me; therefore I will remember you from the land of the Jordan, the heights of Hermon – from Mount Mizar* (Psalm 42:1-6).

David had just come back to the Lord after falling into sin with Bathsheba. Yet he still had to deal with the aftermath of his mistake. God had forgiven him, yet the people despised him. He was losing their confidence. The kingdom was deteriorating and his son was conspiring against him.

Things were quite bleak for David when he wrote this psalm.

He describes his soul as being *downcast within* him. That is an apt description of depression: you feel dejected, your posture reflects it, you talk to people with your eyes lowered. How did David get out of his gloom?

First, he truly repented of his past actions.

David says, "My soul pants after you, O God." He is thirsty to know more of the Lord. As bad as his failure was, he had made a 180-degree "about face."

Second, he emptied his soul to the Father.

Do not keep the depression hidden from God. He knows it already; you might as well tell the Lord what you are experiencing. You will feel much better.

> ***Worship and praise is the antidote God prescribes for hopelessness.***

David wrote, "Men say to me all day long, 'Where is your God?' These things I remember as I pour out my soul."

Third, the psalmist had lost hope in God.

David wrote, "Why are you downcast, O my soul? Why so disturbed within me? Put your hope in God."

Be honest with yourself: are you downtrodden because you have lost faith that things will turn around? David chose to put his trust in the Lord. Then he added, "For I will yet praise him."

Worship and praise is the antidote God prescribes for hopelessness.

REAL JOY!

God's Word tells us to *"Rejoice in the Lord always. I will say it again: Rejoice!"* (Philippians 4:4).

How often are you to praise Him? You know the answer: *Always!* You might say, "I don't feel like expressing joy." Well, the Lord didn't say, "Rejoice, only if you feel like it." He said, "Rejoice always."

This is what gives you the stamina to stand and fight. *The joy of the Lord is your strength* (Nehemiah 8:10).

James wrote, *Consider it pure joy, my brothers, whenever you face trials of many kinds* (James 1:2).

Pure joy is not happiness. The word derives from the word "happen." Happiness, therefore, is based on what is taking place.

God says that pure joy occurs even in the midst of trials – even when the car breaks down, when the kids get sick, when the boss cuts your hours, or when your spouse is in a bad mood.

Why is James telling us to count it pure joy whenever we face adversity? Because joy gives you strength to withstand, and when you do, you will overcome.

James continues, *Perseverance must finish its work so that you may be mature and complete, not lacking anything* (v.4). You see, James believes he has *victory* over trials, not acceptance of them. It is by rejoicing that we triumph.

"YET I WILL REJOICE"

I love the words written by the prophet Habakkuk. *Though the fig tree does not bud and there are no grapes on the vines, though the olive crops fail and the fields produce no food, though there are no sheep in the pen and no cattle in the stalls* (Habakkuk 3:17).

It sounds as though this man had great problems.

Wait! It's not as bad as it seems. One simple three-letter word changes the outlook. That word is "Yet!"

Habakkuk did not surrender to his difficulties. Instead, he looked up to heaven and exclaimed, *Yet I will rejoice in the Lord, I will be joyful in God my Savior (v 18).*

Here is *why* he can rejoice. *The Sovereign Lord is my strength; he makes my feet like the feet of a deer, he enables me to go on the heights* (v.19).

Habakkuk had no intention of *staying* defeated. He may look vanquished, but he was not going to remain that way.

The difference between the person who is defeated and one who is victorious is the quality we mentioned earlier - attitude. The prophet had an attitude of gratitude!

Even though his life was in a downward spiral - no fruit, no crops, no sheep, no cattle - yet he rejoiced.

In today's jargon, Habakkuk might have said it this way: "Though my refrigerator is empty, I'm down to my last penny, my body is frail and the pain persists; though my children are on drugs, and my spouse does not appreciate me, yet I will praise the Lord. I will be joyful in God my Savior."

Regardless of the circumstances, you can lift your hands in praise!

When you eliminate the first two reasons for depression - sin and attitude - you are ready to deal with the demons that can be at the heart of the problem.

CHAPTER 8

HOPE FOR THE DEPRESSED

Derek Prince seemed to have everything going for him. He had a good education, made a decent living, and was a very moral person. He was a born again Christian and was pastoring a church near the center of London, England.

From every outward appearance he was a successful minister. Each week he would witness at least one conversion or miracle of healing in his church. Yet, he had an inner feeling of disappointment.

Prince felt an inaudible voice whisper to him, *Others may succeed, but you won't.* His soul matched the gray surroundings of London. The skies were gray. The houses were gray. The people even seemed gray. Even worse, his soul was gray. He could not shake this inner sense of gloom.

He tried every means to get rid of his depression. He faithfully read his Bible, fasted once a week and devoted himself to intense prayer. Yet despite all of his efforts, he never felt any better. He began to grow hopeless over his situation.

His answer came in 1953. He was reading the first part of Isaiah 61 when the phrase, "the spirit of heaviness" forcefully struck his consciousness. There it was - his condition. He had that same spirit weighing on his life.

THE MIST WAS GONE!

Derek Prince thought to himself, *Could it be that the force I am struggling with is not a part of me, but an actual alien being?* He recalled the term "familiar spirit" (Leviticus 19:31). Was it possible that such a spirit had attached itself to members of his family and had finally moved down to him?

He recalled his father's bout with depression. For the most part, his dad behaved like a gentleman, yet there were rare times when something would upset him so much, he would shut out the members of his family. For twenty-four hours he would sit in stone silence. Then, for no apparent reason, he would return to normal.

After reading this scripture, Prince had a new revelation. He no longer viewed his depression as being part of his personality. He saw it as being a demon that had come to make his ministry ineffective. The only issue now was how to deal with this spirit. He remembered the passage, *And it shall come to pass, that whosoever shall call on the name of the Lord shall be delivered* (Joel 2: 32 KJV).

He quickly put the verse into practice, praying, "Lord, You've shown me that I have been oppressed by a spirit of heaviness, but You have promised in Your Word that if I call on Your name, I shall be delivered. So I'm calling on You now to deliver me, in the name of Jesus."

No sooner did he utter this prayer when he felt something like a gigantic vacuum cleaner come over him and suck away the gray mist. While this went on, the pressure in his chest was forcefully released. "Ugh!" he gasped.

God miraculously intervened. He was delivered!

In his book, *They Shall Expel Demons*, Prince writes, "Suddenly everything around me seemed brighter. I felt as if a heavy burden had been lifted from my shoulders. I was free!"

"I felt as if a heavy burden had been lifted from my shoulders. I was free!"

THE ROOT OF YOUR CONDITION

You may relate to Derek Prince's experience. Perhaps you have this inexplicable and yet unexplained depression. You do not have any hidden sin that has not been confessed. Nothing terrible has gone wrong in your life, yet the oppression is there. It's real.

This dark cloud causes you to become pessimistic – you lose your zest for life and worry that everything is about to go wrong. It could well be that the root of your condition is demonic.

Don't wait! Call on the Lord and see what He can do. Your deliverance may differ from that of Derek Prince, but it will be real. You might need to have someone pray over you, or you may have the faith to pray alone and find release. God is sovereign! He can perform miracles with, or without, people praying for you.

Recently, a doctor in my church was suffering from depression and could not explain why this was happening to him. He had every comfort of life anyone could ever want. Then one day, I was teaching on the topic of deliverance when he suddenly realized his problem was a demon.

The man never thought an agent of the devil could attack him. After some prodding from his friends, he came forward for prayer. He sobbed as I laid hands on him. I spoke to the spirit of heaviness resting on him, and asked it to leave. Instantly, he was freed! – and has not suffered from depression since.

A Helmet of Hope

If Satan can trick you into believing that God has not restored you, then he can bring his evil spirits back into your life.

Once you are delivered, don't let down your spiritual guard. Satan will attempt to make a return visit. That's what happened to Dr. Prince. He had to continually fight off the attacks of the enemy until Satan eventually gave up.

If Satan can deceive you into believing that God has not really restored you, then he can bring his evil spirits back into your life. Make a stand against the enemy.

Put on the *hope of salvation as a helmet* (1Thessalonians 5:8). Remember, a helmet covers your head – your mind.

You can suffer an injury on any part of your body, but a head injury often is the most severe. That's why headgear is mandated for almost all sports. The same is true spiritually; you must protect your mind. The weapon God has given you is "hope" – the positive expectation that the Lord will work out His good plan for your life.

You can always tell when someone is hopeful. They are watching with great anticipation for the answer. If they are waiting for an important letter, they are looking out their window for the postman. If they are anxious for their loved one to call, they sit by the phone, expecting every ring to be that person.

When you are filled with hope, you believe every day will be a miracle. "Somehow, God is coming through for me," you say. If you are sick, you attend a healing service. You don't stay home and complain, "I probably won't get healed." No, you go expecting a miracle.

There is wonder working power in hope!

CHAPTER 9

THE SPIRIT OF JEALOUSY

Keep all the doors to demons locked and bolted. Remember King Saul? A "tormenting spirit" filled him with fear and caused his depression.

A closer look at the story reveals the open entryway for a demon. The door was jealousy.

Saul was handsome and people adored him. He was an impressive young man without equal among the Israelites – *a head taller than any of the others* (2 Samuel 9:2). If there was anyone who did not need to be jealous, Saul was that person.

Later in his reign young David joined his ranks. David killed Goliath and led Israel on triumphant invasions against their enemies.

David earned an enviable reputation in Israel. So great, in fact, that the young women orchestrated a dance tune with the refrain, *Saul has slain his thousands, and David his tens of thousands* (1 Samuel 19:7).

This hit song did not settle well with the king: *Saul was*

very angry; this refrain galled him. "They have credited David with tens of thousands." he thought, "but me with only thousands. What more can he get but the kingdom?" And from that time on Saul kept a jealous eye on David (1 Samuel 18:8-9).

Saul's insecurity and envy opened him to demons. As the following verse records, *The next day an evil spirit from God came forcefully upon Saul. He was prophesying in his house, while David was playing the harp, as he usually did. Saul had a spear in his hand and he hurled it, saying to himself, "I'll pin David to the wall," But David eluded him twice* (vv.10-11).

Notice the correlation between Saul's jealousy and the evil spirit. Such spirits feed on envy.

IT'S AN IDOL

Demons can provoke resentment. That fact is made plain in Ezekiel. *He stretched out what looked like a hand and took me by the hair of my head. The Spirit lifted me up between earth and heaven and in visions of God he took me to Jerusalem, to the entrance to the north gate of the inner court, where the idol that provokes jealousy stood* (Ezekiel 8:3).

An idol is a demon, and can arouse envy.

An idol is a demon (see again 1 Corinthians 10:20), and can arouse envy.

This is what happened to Saul. He allowed the temptation of jealousy to lodge in his soul. Consequently, an evil spirit was able to enter and torment him, causing him to attack David. I have seen this duplicated in the lives of many sincere people.

THE JEWELS

Never underestimate the insidious power of jealousy.

I heard about a woman who was making arrangements with an artist to sit for her portrait. She said to him, "Although I have only a few items of jewelry, I want this painting to show me wearing diamond rings and earrings, an emerald brooch, and a multi-strand necklace of pearls that must look like they are priceless."

"I can paint those easily," replied the artist. "But do you mind telling me why, when apparently you do not particularly care for jewelry?"

"Well," said the woman, "if I die first, and my husband marries again, I want the second wife to go out of her mind trying to find where he hid the jewels!"

We may smile at this story, but jealousy is no laughing matter. It has a history of ruining families, businesses, churches and governments. It can torment your soul like nothing else – and worse – you may not even know you have it. The disease can be hidden.

THE DIAGNOSIS

These feelings must be diagnosed. If left undetected, they can fester permanent wounds. How can you tell if you are afflicted? Here are three ways:

First: You are afraid of losing someone's love, affection or favor.

Someone more talented than you joins the praise and worship team in your church. Your position as lead vocalist is threatened. Instead of being happy that more talent is available to sing God's praises, you find your fear begins to unconsciously cause you to look for faults with the new singer. You point out their flaws to the pastor: "They do not seem spiritual enough." "They show up late." "They have too much pride."

What is happening? Your jealousy is manifested in fear, and so you do what you can to hold your position. You have your own form of "throwing spears."

Second: You are angry, unhappy or depressed because of what someone else has.

Your next door neighbor just purchased a brand new luxury automobile. You plaster on a smile as he pulls into his driveway. You compliment him on his car, while secretly you are unhappy. You look at your own car and are envious. Suddenly, your sedan seems outdated - and you don't enjoy driving it anymore.

Perhaps your son failed to make the little league team, yet your best friend's child was chosen. How do you feel about the situation? Are you really happy? Or do you think, "He's not any better than my boy! If he made the team, my son definitely should have made it!"

The next time you have dinner with your best friend, you no longer seem to enjoy his company. What has taken place? Your jealousy is manifested in unhappiness over what you have, or anger over what someone else has. You begin to dislike the person who has received what you feel you deserved. It is a spirit of covetousness.

Third: You are careful to guard or keep what you have.

You are proud of your husband, but there is one woman you think has her eye on him. You say to yourself, "I can't stand her!"

Your husband surprises you and takes you out for a romantic evening – a new restaurant you have wanted to visit for months. You sit down at your table, but across the room is that "other woman."

"Why is she here?" you angrily ask your husband in a tone higher than a whisper. Do you enjoy your meal, or are you seething? Are you angry because you fear you might lose him? The evening is a disaster.

You say to yourself, "I can't stand her!"

What has happened? Your jealousy is manifested in your desire to guard your husband, and you become overprotective. You pretend to care for your husband, yet it is really *you* that is the focus of your concern.

This occurs with pastors as well. You have carefully scheduled an important event at your church, then you hear another church has announced a really spectacular production.

What is your reaction? On purpose, you make sly remarks to your congregation about the carnality of "certain" churches. You want to make sure you don't lose members of your congregation to a competitor.

Is this showing God's love for your church? No. You pretend to be concerned, but really, you are in a mode of self-protection.

"YOU'VE GOT TO BE KIDDING!"

When people are confronted with the sin of jealousy, they usually deny they possess it. "What! Me Jealous? You've got to be kidding!"

There is good reason why people won't admit they have

the green-eyed monster. They often don't know what it actually is, since there is a misconception about this sin.

Don't confuse jealousy with inferiority.

Don't confuse jealousy with inferiority. The Bible says, "God is a jealous God" (see Exodus 20:5), and we all know He does not feel inferior to anyone. Jealousy is a right that only God can claim, because no one is better or greater than He. No one else has the *right* to be jealous.

AN EMOTION?

What we are talking about is not an emotion like fear or depression. When we are fearful we might tremble, become nervous or feel a sinking pit inside our stomach. It's something we can all relate to. Depression is the same. We feel downcast, discouraged, empty; our faces show it.

There are other feelings, such as guilt and resentment we are familiar with. But jealousy doesn't have its own unique emotion. This is why it is hard to pinpoint the exact moment it is present.

Rather than producing its own symptoms, jealousy borrows other emotions. For example, no one would dispute the fact that Cain was envious of his brother, Able. Look at the passage: *But Abel brought fat portions from some of the firstborn of his flock. The Lord looked with favor on Abel and his offerings, but on Cain and his offerings he did not look with favor. So Cain was very angry, and his face was downcast* (Genesis 4:4-5).

Later, Cain murdered his brother. What was at the root of Cain's problem? Jealousy. Yet scripture never uses this word to describe Cain. Instead, the Bible depicts a certain emotion that Cain felt: *anger*. It tells us his facial expression: *his face was downcast*. No mention, however, of his jealousy.

The reason is because envy is the root of the fruit of many negative feelings - such as anger, depression, fear, anxiety and resentment. The emotions were obviously seen in Cain, but God wanted him to recognize them, and their source. *Why are you angry? Why is your face downcast?* (v.6).

FACING THE FACTS

God did not accuse Cain of being angry or depressed. Rather, He asked the question "Why?"

Cain *knew* he was upset and recognized the fact that his spirits were low. "Sure, God, I know that!" However, the Lord wanted Cain to face the *reason* for his feelings.

It was obvious that Cain was extremely jealous of his brother. By not facing the cause of his emotional problems, he started down the path of self-destruction.

The same was true of Saul. He never acknowledged the cause of his resentment toward David. Young David had not done anything to wrong Saul. He served him faithfully and never conspired against him, yet Saul hated him. Why? Because he was enviousness.

THE CONFLICT

Perhaps you are beginning to recognize a similar problem in your own life. It's true that jealousy affects every type of relationship, from marriage to siblings to employees to church members, Look how it destroyed the bond between Joseph and his brothers, how it affected Rachel and Leah, Jacob and Esau.

It has even sparked wars. *What causes fights and quarrels*

among you? Don't they come from your desires that battle within you? You want something but don't get it. You kill and covet, but you cannot have what you want (James 4:1-2).

The long-simmering Israeli and Palestinian conflict is fueled by jealousy. Certain people feel entitled to more than their counterparts.

Jealousy is based on coveting what another person has. And that is a sin. James continues, *Do ye think that the scripture saith in vain, The spirit that dwelleth in us lusteth to envy?* (James 4:5 KJV).

Envy and jealousy are used synonymously, but technically they are different. Envy involves only two parties – you want what someone else has. Jealousy can involve more than two. In the Greek text there is only one word for both terms – it is the word *qana'*.

Jealousy was the basic reason the leaders of Jerusalem crucified Christ.

TRAGIC CONSEQUENCES

The Bible is replete with warnings against jealousy. It tells us the tragic effects this sin will have on us. Yet we don't seem to care. We are headstrong, and it leads toward destruction. *A heart at peace gives life to the body, but envy rots the bones* (Proverbs 14:30).

Jealousy can ruin your health!

It couldn't be more plain. Jealousy can ruin your health!

Here is another biblical caution: *Resentment kills a fool, and envy slays the simple. I myself have seen a fool taking root, but suddenly his house was cursed* (Job 5:2-3).

Just when everything is going well, *boom!* Something awful happens. You struggle to understand why God allowed this, but little do you know that *envy slays the simple.* You were *taking* root, but suddenly your *house was cursed.* Your children were destroyed – all because of jealousy.

There have been many successful people that seemed invincible. They seemed so secure and rooted! Yet their world crumbled because of their envious nature.

SOMETHING BETTER

If you sincerely desire to overcome jealousy, learn to stand in respect and fear of the Lord. Here is what the Word declares: *Do not let your heart envy sinners, but always be zealous for the fear of the Lord. There is surely a future hope for you, and your hope will not be cut off* (Proverbs 23:17-18).

Recognize the fact that God is watching how you treat others. It is natural to feel certain emotions when others get blessed or when you feel your position is threatened. You are human, and will feel anxiety, depression and perhaps even anger. You must not act on these emotions whether in word or deed.

Do not speak evil of others when they are blessed. Rejoice with them. Purpose to live at peace with others.

Believe there is hope for you, and it *will not be cut off.* God has not forgotten you. He has a great plan for your future.

- Father, your son will find his talents.
- Wife, God will protect your husband – even without your help.
- Pastor, your church will grow in His time.

Should things not turn out as you planned, rest assured, God has something better in store. Don't become discouraged when it seems the Lord has passed you by, because He has not. He will still bless you.

You do not need to envy anyone. Ask for God's deliverance. By His miraculous power, jealousy will vanish.

Part III

Spiritual Diseases

CHAPTER 10

CAN THE HUMAN SPIRIT BECOME SICK?

There is much controversy over the topic of the human spirit, especially the issue as to whether or not the born again human spirit can become sick. Opinions do not count. The Word of God answers the question.

Some query whether or not we even *have* a spirit. Many see mankind as only mind and body. Yet there is much more to us. We have a *spirit*. This explains why we humans are the only creatures that are spiritual. Animals are not religious – it is a uniquely human institution.

Anthropologists have theories about the evolution of religious belief. They speculate that seed comes from the desire for immortality. However, that does not answer *why* we crave to be immortal. They say, "Man fears the unseen, so he invents theories about God, angels, and demons." Again, this does not explain *why* man can *believe* in the unseen much less fear it.

Critics of the creation account of the Bible admit that mankind has the highest intelligence of any creatures, yet they put themselves in a quandary when they dismiss the notion that man has a spirit made in the image of God. Even the most skeptical must admit that mankind is unique from the animal kingdom. We are different because of two things: we have a soul *and a spirit.*

We are different because of two things: we have a soul and a spirit.

THREE GREAT NEEDS

The needs of mankind are threefold: physical, soul and spiritual. Or to put it into contemporary terms: biological, psychological, and spiritual.

Consider the three most essential *physical* needs of all creatures, both man and animals: eating, sleeping, and sex. Unlike animals, humans approach these needs in a totally different fashion. We see them as both psychological and spiritual.

For example, animals eat when they are hungry. Humans however eat for social reasons as well as hunger. We have developed human rituals around food, and are the only creatures that cook and season what we eat. We do not simply take the food and place it into our mouths. No! We put it on plates, eat with forks, and dine with other people. Why? To meet our psychological needs.

However, we can also use these rituals to meet our spiritual requirements. At the dinner table, for example, we may bow our heads and give thanks to God. We pray over our food – something animals don't do. Some religions take the ritual further, believing we partake of divinity when we eat. The bottom line is that humans not only eat to serve biological necessities, but also psychological and spiritual needs.

We're Unique!

The same can be said about sleep. Animals sleep when they get tired. As humans, we *schedule* our sleep times. We do not simply lie down where we are; rather, we make a bed and put covers on it. We may even change clothes before we retire. The routine is clearly different than other creatures.

Sleep can be spiritual. We have dreams at night and often interpret them as possible words from God, omens, or warnings about the future. Many take their dreams seriously.

Even sex is different for humans. One obvious difference is clothing. No animals put on clothes to cover their procreative parts. We do. Of course, people could argue that Adam and Eve were naked and they had a spirit that told them what to do. Remember, however, they were also husband and wife. It was *sin* that brought shame.

Another thing that separates us is the fact that humans are the only ones who make love face to face. This meets a psychological need. Also, animals have sex in public – they engage in such behavior when they want to, and don't care who is watching. Uniquely, humans close the door and have sex privately. (Unfortunately, pornographers have turned sex into an animalistic act, but this is not the norm.)

Mankind can even make sex a spiritual act. How? By making a lifetime commitment through a vow of marriage.

No animals marry. We do, and *not* for simple psychological reasons, but for spiritual reasons. Something tells us that when we are married "God has joined" us in holy matrimony.

As you can tell, man is more than mind and body, he is a spirit made in God's image.

OUR CONNECTION TO GOD

The human spirit is the umbilical cord connecting us to God – making us aware of the Creator's existence. It is the God-side of us, the part that makes us *godly*, like the Father.

All the good that we do comes from this source. Unfortunately, evil can also proceed out of an unregenerate spirit. As Jesus said, *The good man brings good things out of the good stored up in him, and the evil man brings evil things out of the evil stored up in him* (Matthew 12:35).

The human spirit also gives us the conscious awareness of eternity. *God has set eternity in the hearts of men* (Ecclesiastes 3:11).

As much as atheists and agnostics try, I believe they can't shake off the feelings that they will live forever. Nearly every religion believes in life after death. They derive their belief from the sensations of the human spirit – which makes us aware of eternity.

This also helps us contact the invisible world of the spirit. The supernatural phenomenon claimed by some as "out of body experiences," "contacting the dead," and "knowing the future" are really products of the human spirit.

WHAT THE BIBLE FORBIDS

Mediums are called "spiritists" in the Bible. These people

operate through their own spirits. Unfortunately, they are unaware they are not contacting human spirits but *familiar* spirits. This is why the Bible forbids contact with the dead. God says about those who die, *They are now dead, they live no more; those departed spirits do not rise* (Isa 26:14). Departed spirits do not contact the living, so the living cannot contact *them*.

Intuitive feelings, though not logical, are fruits of the human spirit. We feel something is about to happen, but we have no tangible proof. We call it "a gut feeling."

If those premonitions never came to pass, we would discount them, but often they do come true. Those feelings are human in nature.

Our spirits contain our motives - not a product of the soul, but of the human spirit. The Bible says that God *will expose the motives of men's hearts* (1 Corinthians 4:5). The conscience is the voice of the human spirit. Though we may try to rationalize our behavior, the voice of our spirit speaks out.

Our spirits contain our motives – not a product of the soul, but of the human spirit.

PURIFICATION!

No Christian minister doubts the depravity of the human spirit. It is capable of all kinds of atrocities. As one of the biblical prophets has said, *The heart is deceitful above all things and beyond cure* (Jeremiah 17:9).

We know the unregenerate spirit is sick – *beyond cure.* But what about the born-again spirit. Can the regenerated human spirit become sick?

Here is what Paul says concerning this: *Since we have these promises, dear friends, let us purify ourselves from everything that contaminates body and spirit, perfecting holiness out of reverence for God* (2 Corinthians 7:1).

Paul is writing to the believers, and he tells them to cleanse themselves from *everything* that can taint or defile their body and spirit.

THE ANSWER FOR A SICK SPIRIT

There is no argument whether or not the body can be contaminated, so if *it* can get sick, then why not the spirit? Paul would not encourage cleansing of the human spirit if it were always clean. You only need to encourage washing if the object can get dirty. Thus, the human spirit can become polluted and sick.

Let's look again at what Paul said about the three-fold nature of man: *May your whole spirit, soul and body be kept blameless at the coming of our Lord Jesus Christ* (1Thessalonians 5:23). This benediction proves that the spirit needs God's power to be kept blameless.

Theologians do not question whether the body or soul can become sick, yet this passage teaches that the human spirit also needs God's sanctifying work.

The greatest malady is spiritual. God's Word says, *A man's spirit sustains him in sickness* (Proverbs 18:14). Even in infirmity, a man's spirit may be able to nurture him and give him the strength to recover. But what happens when the human spirit is sick? Where will he turn for sustenance and help? A man's body or soul can't heal his spirit.

That is when we must turn to God. Only He can bring complete deliverance.

Chapter 11

The World of the Occult

Somewhere in nearly all of us is a desire to contact the unknown, some "higher power" – something greater, wiser and more powerful than ourselves. People's curiosity causes them to delve into the occult.

The word "occult" comes from a Latin word meaning "concealed or covered over, a secret." It is knowledge of the supernatural kind.

There is nothing intrinsically wrong with this type of knowledge. After all, God Himself imparts knowledge. The real issue is the source. Is it coming from God or some other being?

The Creator made both a natural and a spiritual world. The "natural world" is a tangible universe that can be studied through facts; and the "spiritual world" is an unseen realm that can only be understood properly through *God science*.

Religion, in attempting to explain the world of the

spirit, depends on the conscience.

The word *conscience* is derived from two words *con* meaning "with" and *science* meaning "a branch of knowledge dealing with a body of facts showing the operation of general laws." Science deals with math, astronomy, chemistry, literature, etc. Conscience, then, deals with questions that science cannot answer.

Religion is *divine* science, and it should work along side with *natural* science - neither should compete with the other. Science can't answer religious questions, and religion was not meant to answer scientific questions.

Although researchers can study objects and events, there are many things they cannot test. Science has its limitations. For example, it cannot measure a mother's love for her children - or the difference between good and evil.

History can tell you what Hitler did, but it cannot answer whether or not he was "evil." Good and evil are issues for religion to grapple with. They are questions of conscience.

WHICH VIEW?

This brings us to the issue of true religion. There are basically three religious views about God:

1. Polytheistic - belief in many gods.
2. Pantheistic - belief that god is in the elements.
3. Monotheistic - belief in one God that is over the worlds.

Prior to Christianity, polytheism was the predominate view. People in those times believed that certain forces, like the wind or sun, were spirit beings. They worshiped them as gods.

This theory is still widespread through certain parts of the world such as India. Hindus are polytheistic and comprise the largest religion in this group. Some of these practices have spread to the West. Yoga, for example, is a branch of Hinduism, as are the concepts of reincarnation and Karma.

Pantheism is the belief that God and the whole universe are one and the same, and that the Creator does not exist as a separate spirit. Witches are often pantheistic. They view objects as part of the divine energy of God. They like to use objects such as crystals to channel supernatural energy.

God specifically warns against delving into the spiritual world without His approval.

The predominate world-view is monotheism - a belief that one God created the whole universe and He reigns over all, much like a builder is over the development of a project. The builder is not the bricks or cement, rather the designer and constructor of the building.

The two largest world religions are monotheistic: Christianity and Islam. Judaism, which predates both religions, is also monotheistic. Through the Hebrew scriptures, God specifically warns against exploring the spiritual world without His approval.

SPIRITUAL DECEPTION

Here is what God said to the children of Israel: *When you enter the land the Lord your God is giving you, do not learn to imitate the detestable ways of the nations there. Let no one be found among you who sacrifices his son or daughter in the fire, who practices divination or sorcery, interprets omens, engages in witchcraft, or casts spells, or who is a medium or spiritist or who consults the dead. Anyone who does these things is detestable to the Lord, and because of these detestable practices the Lord your God will drive out those nations before you. You must be blameless before the Lord your God* (Deuteronmy 18:9-13).

God has placed within us the longing to know the realm of the spirit.

God has placed within us the longing to know the realm of the spirit, but His archenemy, Satan, has invented ways to divert people into deceptive – evil systems that bring them into bondage to himself.

These misleading practices can take countless forms, but the standard name for them all is the occult. In ancient Israel these were called divination, sorcery, witchcraft, casting spells, and consulting the dead. This description may be thousands of years old, yet it sounds like what Hollywood is promoting today.

Movies, television and video games are making the occult attractive – or at the very least *benign.*

Be warned; the occult is harmful. That is why God gives such clear warnings against it. You see psychic hotline programs with a disclaimer at the bottom of the screen: *For entertainment only*. I believe it is *dangerous* entertainment.

IS IT REALLY WRONG?

I can hear some people sigh, "C'mon, pastor. You don't

really believe those things are harmful, do you?"

Yes! This is exactly why I am teaching on this subject. The world, including Christians, has become desensitized to the occult.

Consider the stern warning: *The acts of the sinful nature are obvious: sexual immorality, impurity and debauchery; idolatry and witchcraft; hatred, discord, jealousy, fits of rage, selfish ambition, dissensions, factions and envy; drunkenness, orgies, and the like. I warn you, as I did before, that those who live like this will not inherit the kingdom of God.* (Galatians 5:19-21).

Look at the list carefully. The offenses are grouped in four categories (divided by semi-colons).

- The first group is *sexual* sins.
- The second group is *occult* sins.
- The third group is *hate* sins.
- The fourth group is *unruly* sins.

Depending on your background, certain categories are sinful to you, while others are not. However, according to the Word, they all *are* iniquities.

Liberals often lobby against hate sins, such as racism. Conservatives often lobby against sexual sins. While both often debate with each other, the truth is we should be united against all forms of evil. We should not pick and choose which are really wrong. Sin is wrong, period!

We are not given the choice by God to declare what is good or evil. God tells us – and our choice is to agree or disagree with Him.

I have decided not to be influenced by the current culture. God is the judge, and no one else. He declares that all sin is evil.

IS GOD ANGRY?

One of the categories listed by Paul is the occult. He specifically mentions idolatry and witchcraft. By covering these two occult sins, he condemns the two other forms of religion: polytheism and pantheism. These two religions use deceptive methods to search the unknown realm of the spirit. They often use their unregenerate spirit to contact gods, or their god.

When people try to tap into the spiritual world in an unauthorized manner, they open themselves to demons.

When people attempt to tap into the spiritual world in an unauthorized manner, they unknowingly open themselves to demons. This is clear in the Word: *The sacrifices of pagans are offered to demons, not to God* (1 Corinthians 10:20). It is a reference to offering sacrifices to idols, and the occult has its origin in idolatry.

God is *angry* with these practices. Here is the reaction of the Lord to a wicked king by the name of Manasseh: *He sacrificed his sons in the fire in the Valley of Ben Hinnom, practiced sorcery, divination and witchcraft, and consulted mediums and spiritists. He did much evil in the eyes of the Lord, provoking him to anger* (2 Chronicles 33:6).

Battle for the Mind

An example of deliverance from spirits that have their roots in the occult is found in the book of Acts: *Once when we were going to the place of prayer, we were met by a slave girl who had a spirit by which she predicted the future. She earned a great deal of money for her owners by fortune-telling. This girl followed Paul and the rest of us, shouting, "These men are servants of the Most High God, who are telling you the way to be saved." She kept this up for many days. Finally Paul became so troubled that he turned around and said to the spirit, "In the name of Jesus Christ I command you to come out of her!" At that moment the spirit left her. When the owners of the slave girl realized that their hope of making money was gone, they seized Paul and Silas and dragged them into the marketplace to face the authorities* (Acts 16:16-19).

This young girl had a rare talent to predict the future. The Bible says that *a spirit* gave her this ability, but when Paul drove out the spirit, she lost this power.

The real problem was that she generated a great deal of money for her owners. Since early times, fortune telling has been a lucrative business. The proliferation of psychic hotlines today still gives evidence to this fact.

Something worth noticing about this girl is that she appeared to advocate Christianity. She shouted, "These men are servants of the Most High God, who are telling you the way to be saved."

Some Christians are fooled about the occult when fortune tellers or psychics appear to talk about the God of the Bible. They *sound* Christian, but their practice is occultic. Paul was not taken in by that kind of phony witness for the Lord. Don't you be either!

Finally, in this story there was a battle for the minds of

the community. The owners of the girl had Paul arrested and eventually he left the city.

I have observed how hard those who practice the occult can be on Christians. It is a never-ending fight that is bolstered by the media. Yet, as Paul showed, the work of the Holy Spirit is greater than the power of Satan.

THE DISEASE OF DECEPTION

There has been a revival of witchcraft in America, especially among the young people.

Harry Potter books and motion pictures have heightened the interest in many children to learn about magic. *The Sixth Sense* has made others curious concerning contacting the dead. Television programs such as *Crossing Over with John Edward* have brought seances into our living rooms.

Many people see witchcraft as innocent and harmless. I admit that only a minority of people will turn to the occult after viewing those programs and movies, but even *one* is too many.

When people practice witchcraft and seances, their spirits contact demons – which leads to Satan's deceit.

It is the deception that is the disease. That is what causes people to grow cold toward the Lord. They open themselves to other doctrines that confuse their understanding of the Bible. Eventually they deny what is essential to be saved and may even lose their salvation.

You do not actually have to be a witch to be deceived; you only need to *listen* to witches. Deception is like a contagious virus, passed onto others who open themselves to these witches and spiritists.

IT'S NOT CHILD'S PLAY

It is not by coincidence that much of the occult is targeted toward children. Young people are more susceptible to these things than adults. Sadly, when a child is deceived, the error is ingrained on their spirit, and causes them to become hardened toward the gospel.

> *It is not by coincidence that much of the occult is targeted toward children.*

As a preteen and teenager, I would often explore the occult. I played with the ouija board, the eight ball, tarot cards, palm reading, biorhythm and horoscopes. They seemed innocent enough, yet little did I know what I was plunging into.

One day, my cousins and I were playing with the ouija board, asking it questions and then waiting for the answers. We asked a particular question about when we would die. All of a sudden, we heard a loud sound that startled us. After trying to stay calm, we jumped up, ran into the kitchen and found a broken plate on the floor. It fell out of the cabinet all by itself. We unanimously agreed to get rid of the ouija board!

I can't explain what happened. I don't know if the devil threw that plate down or whether God tried to scare us from dabbling in the occult – all I know it was spooky!

There is a supernatural element found in such practices. Sure, sometimes there are fakes who lure people into the unknown, yet other times there are unexplainable events that happen.

The important decision is to stay away from witchcraft, sorcery, divination and other occult practices. They will contaminate your spirit.

The Bible says, *do not give the devil a foothold* (Ephesians 4:27). A foothold is a small opening to a door – and that is all an intruder needs to force his way inside.

The devil looks for any opportunity to gain entry into your life – and the occult can be that crack in the door. Don't give him any ground.

CHAPTER 12

BREAKING FREE!

In one school a group of girls began playing with an ouija board just as an experiment. A message from the board said, "Within a week one of you will be dead."

Just as it foretold, one of the girls died in a car accident.

It is tragic to see the effects of the occult. Those who participate give an open invitation for Satan to bring adversity to their lives.

You might have been entangled in things mystical and now you want to break free. Let me assure you that God will forgive you for any involvement. He will set you free from the power that Satan may have over your life.

How do you find this liberty? As we learned in discussing idols in Chapter Three, you must rid your life of any objects associated with evil.

Follow this example from the Word: *Many of those who believed now came and openly confessed their evil deeds. A number who had practiced sorcery brought their scrolls together and burned them publicly. When they calculated the value of the scrolls, the total came to fifty thousand drachmas* (Acts 19:18-19).

These people did two things: first, they openly confessed their evil ways; second, they burned their scrolls. They divested themselves of any association with sorcery.

Some individuals seem concerned over book burnings, but it is thoroughly scriptural. You need to take whatever objects are connected with the occult and destroy them. Either throw them in the fire or a garbage can.

A chill ran up my spine when I heard the accounts of people who made the decision to burn their evil items. One testified, "I heard screams when I threw my occult paraphernalia in the flames."

"GOOD" WITCHES?

At the age of eighteen, the Word of God convicted me that I needed to get rid of my collection of comic books. As I flipped through them, for the first time I noticed many references to the occult. I saw "good" witches casting spells for the benefit of mankind. I thought, *How weird to portray witches as being good.*

I came to the conclusion that I wanted nothing to do with witchcraft. I took my stash of comic books to my backyard. I dug a hole and began to bury them. My next door neighbor noticed what I was doing and begged, "Don't throw those away! Why don't you give them to me?"

I refused. Why should I pass on demons to others? Perhaps you think I was too extreme, but I simply followed the example of the Christians at Ephesus in the Bible.

Take inventory of your household. What articles of clothing, books, videos, and games do you have that are associated with Satan? Get rid of them. That's how you close the door on the enemy.

Ask God to forgive you and receive His pardon. Renounce any involvement you have had with witchcraft. Remove yourself from any membership you might have with occultic organizations. If you are connected to a coven, resign and tell them why – and take your stand for Christ.

The word "coven" comes from the word "covenant". If you stay in such a group you are still in covenant with those involved. You must break every evil alliance. Only *you* can do this. Don't leave it to others to renounce Satan for you. You must take the action yourself!

WHAT IS WITCHCRAFT?

Witchcraft is based on magic.

A reliable Internet site called *witches.net* defines witchcraft by saying: In general witchcraft is sorcery, the magical manipulation of the supernormal forces through the use of spells, and the conjuring or invoking of spirits.

Thus, witchcraft is based on magic. It attempts to tamper with supernormal forces such as spirits. If there were only good spirits in the world, there would be little problem with this. Unfortunately, a significant percentage of spirits are evil. So what spirits are they conjuring or trying to manipulate? What "spells" are they using?

A spell is the use of words and objects to induce what the witch desires. They may use such tools as drugs, potions, charms, amulets, magic, spells, incantations, and various forms of music.

The Greek word for witch is *pharmakeia*. As you can tell by the spelling it is similar to pharmacy or drugs. Witches use drugs and potions to attempt to manipulate spirits. The truth is the spirits are manipulating *them!*

To show how antagonistic witchcraft is to the gospel, the ancient requirements for being a witch were:

1. Denial of the Christian Faith.
2. Rebaptism.
3. Swearing allegiance to the devil.
4. Request of the devil to write their name in the book of death.

Today, witchcraft may not require these things, but do you really want to be associated with a religion like this – and one that historically has been so hostile toward Christianity?

MUSIC FROM HELL!

Music plays a prominent role in the occult. I remember in my high school years being really into hard rock. I loved to listen to *Stairway to Heaven* by *Led Zeppelin*. My cousin and I would drive just outside of El Paso, Texas. Then we would play this tape.

When the song reached its climax, I would peel off in

my car, and *zoom*; I was speeding down a newly constructed road. My car would reach speeds of 98 miles an hour before I would have to put on the brakes. As I look back at that madness, I asked myself what contributed to this reckless abandon? No doubt, the music.

Today, Satan infiltrates music with evil themes. No wonder so many of our young people are controlled by the devil. It should not be a surprise that he uses music to entice us, since the Bible says he led the music in heaven before he was expelled.

Later, when I gave my heart to Christ, I took all my worldly albums, including Led Zeppelin's, and crushed them! I broke free from any influence of Satan.

It is time for you to do the same. If you desire freedom from the occult follow these steps:

1. Get rid of any objects associated with the occult.

Gather all the paraphernalia and prepare a burial site. Place them in the grave or burn them.

2. Renounce any involvement with the occult.

If you have been dabbling with ouija boards, psychics, witchcraft, sorcery, mind reading, biorhythm, astrology, or such things, then renounce your involvement. Say out loud, preferably while you are ridding yourself of the items, "I am sorry Lord for offending you by embracing the occult. I repudiate my involvement with ____________________ (be specific and name the objects or people that you used to tap into what is evil). I rebuke all demons and serve them notice that I am serving God and His Son, Jesus Christ, with all of my heart. In Jesus name."

3. Ask God's forgiveness.

God is merciful. He will forgive you if you sincerely ask Him.

4. Take your stand against the enemy.

The devil will not be pleased with your decision. He will fight you and attempt to steal your joy in serving the Lord. He may try to bring great pressure on you, but He cannot win. Satan will flee, and you will be victorious.

Praise God! You can be free from the occult!

Chapter 13

The Trap of Satan

Diseases of the spirit affect your relationship with God. You may be sick in body and still have great communion with the Lord – you may even have some emotional illnesses and still be serving God. However, when your *spirit* is sick, then your relationship with God is suffering.

I have discovered that there is a widespread "spiritual" disease that has become rampant in the body of Christ. This diabolical sickness is extremely contagious. It is also life threatening – especially endangering the spiritual life of God's saints. What is it?

The Bible declares, *Don't have anything to do with foolish and stupid arguments, because you know they produce quarrels. And the Lord's servant must not quarrel; instead, he must be kind to everyone, able to teach, not resentful. Those who oppose him he must gently instruct, in the hope that God will grant them repentance leading them to a knowledge of the truth, and that they will come to their senses and escape from the trap of the devil, who has taken them captive to do his will* (2 Timothy 2:23-26).

Paul talks about a dangerous trap. To those who would argue with men who have foolish reasoning, he says we are to instruct gently *in the hope* that God will grant them repentance, leading them to a knowledge of the truth - and that they will *come to their senses.*

How many people realize the folly of their ways? Very few, but Paul writes hoping that they will. He *hopes*, he does not *believe*.

FEW ESCAPE

The picture is of a hostage - someone who has been taken captive. The odds of people being set free are slim. We get excited when we hear of a prisoner being released.

Heather Mercer and Dayna Curry were taken hostage by the Taliban in Afganisatan for quietly sharing their Christian faith. When they finally escaped from their captors it was front page news and our nation rejoiced.

In this day and age, we are much too accustomed to hearing of bodies found in a shallow grave. It is hard to remain encouraged when someone is reported missing. The same is true when Satan traps God's children.

The Greek word for trap is *pagis*. The history of this term gives some clues to its meaning. The origin is from *Arespagis* (see Acts 17:19). Ares was a strong, fierce fighter who delighted in bloody conflict. He did not simply engage in battle to preserve his nation, he took great pleasure in it. Fighting was his way of life - more enjoyable than a pleasant conversation with a friend. In fact, he would prefer to kill his adversaries than to be kind to his allies.

Like Ares, many derive pleasure in hostility and quarreling. Notice Paul mentioned, "Don't have anything to do with foolish and stupid arguments." Do you see the connection? The trap of Satan causes the person to bicker and fight.

THE LURE

No one falls into a snare on *purpose*. They must be lured into it. Satan baits a trap to entice the unsuspecting.

Every fisherman has his favorite lure. He might not use it right away, trying other things first. However, when nothing seems to work, he pulls out his special bait that few fish can resist.

No one falls into a snare on purpose. They must be lured into it.

How does Satan hook us?

The devil will try everything – tempting you with sex, drugs, money and more. If he succeeds, he may control you for a period of time.

If his attempts fail, he will try to wound you with trials.

There is one lure, however, few can escape. When nothing seems to reel you in, Satan will pull out his most trusted fail-proof enticement. It's so effective that without God's help, few people can resist. The lure is mentioned by Jesus in Luke's gospel: *Then said he unto the disciples, It is impossible but that offences will come: but woe unto him, through whom they come!* (Luke 17:1 KJV).

IT'S A SCANDAL

The Greek word "offences" is the word *skandalon* – a part of a trap that was attached to the bait. In other words, it is the *hook*.

The fishing pole is *pagis*, the hook is *skandalon* – translated as "offences." We are provoked and displeased when someone offends us.

Now you understand why Paul told Timothy to not be *resentful* (2 Timothy 2:24). In other words, don't play the same game as your opponent. Jesus talked about resenting something that is a *scandal* – hence the word *skandalon*.

The outrage may be some action the person believes is wrong. It may be a teaching he believes is heretical. It does not matter what it is, he is offended. Someone has done or said *something* out of order, and now he wants to argue over it.

I have rarely seen an individual like this apologize and come to his or her senses. The person usually goes to the grave still angry.

THE MONKEY TRAP

A National Geographic television special showed the technique poachers use to catch monkeys. They place a banana inside a jar that is tied down. The opening is barely wide enough for the monkey to stick his hand in. When he grabs the banana, it is impossible for him to take out his hand *with* the banana.

When the poachers arrive, the monkey sees them and knows his life is in danger, yet he does not want to let go of the banana. He will scream at the top of his lungs, but still hangs on!

What cost the monkey his freedom? *A banana!*

We humans are not so bright, either. We become offended over something our brother said or did, and we refuse to let go of the offense. The devil approaches, but instead of releasing the issue, we become angry and protest even louder. Eventually, Satan throws us into a prison of our own making.

Eventually, Satan throws us into a prison of our own making.

IT WILL HAPPEN

Jesus said, "It is impossible but that offenses will come." They will *always* arrive.

It's useless to pretend that you will get through life with no one offending you. It will happen. The question is, what will you do when it occurs? Will you take the lure or will you escape?

Jesus, speaking to His disciples, guaranteed they would be affronted and wronged. *Then saith Jesus unto them, All ye shall be offended because of me this night: for it is written, I will smite the shepherd, and the sheep of the flock shall be scattered abroad* (Matthew 26:31 KJV).

No one was excluded!

The people - even some of His followers - were offended because of Jesus. They were troubled because He challenged their man-made plans.

HURT FEELINGS

I have come to the conclusion that if Jesus offended all of His followers, then surely I am going have a few church members take issue with me!

I am not alone. Pastors throughout the world constantly deal with people who are disgruntled and upset. There are always those who disagree with doctrines and decisions.

Jesus never sinned, yet the apostles found fault with Him. One denied knowing the Lord, another betrayed Him. They abandoned Him in His time of need.

As I told a friend, "If all my offended members had stayed in our congregation, we would be a mega-church!"

Jesus never sinned, yet the apostles found something wrong with him.

I'm sure other pastors would agree. The number one reason people leave a church is because of hurt feelings. Let's stop pretending it is because of some other cause. They may give a variety of excuses: "I'm not being fed." "The praise and worship is not anointed." "The children's ministry lacks facilities."

In reality, something else is bothering them. They are hurt, even bruised by the words or actions of another individual. So they leave the church – yet that is not the solution. Letting go of the offense is the cure.

WILL THEY BITE?

Satan rarely uses an "offense" on babes in Christ. They are too easy a prey for this special lure. He will find other things to drag their spirits down. This hook is for the *super*-saints.

I know from experience that it is more difficult to catch the *bigger* fish. It's no trouble pulling in the small ones, yet the big ones don't seem to bite. And if they do, they are a struggle to reel in.

The same is true for the bait called *offense.* Few new believers are snared by it. They are much too excited about the Lord to get bogged down with petty things:

- They think the pastor is the greatest preacher to ever grace the pulpit.
- The music to them is heavenly.
- The deacons are people to be respected.

However, when some individuals attend the same church for an extended period, things seem to change. They notice that the pastor is *human* and makes mistakes. What a revelation!

The babe in Christ never noticed it, but the *spiritual* man has *discernment*. God is using him, after all, to straighten out all the sins of the church. He is qualified, you know!

CATCHING THE "BIG ONE"

If you are a seasoned saint who has fallen for the lure of offense, you are not alone. Who else did you think Satan was trying to catch? Since you have grown so much in Christ, he is afraid of you. Nothing he does seems to work, so he pulls out his trusted hook, and *pow!* You're caught. What snared you? You saw a fault in the church and lost all reasoning – you may even deny that you were a part of *that* congregation.

This may seem harsh, but in truth you are no different than Peter. Worse, you may be like Judas; even betraying those leaders who helped you grow. You hurt others through gossip and try to entice people to leave the church.

Why have you done this? Because you have seen a weakness in the man of God, carnality in the musicians and ego in the elders. The truth is, you are offended.

Seeds of Betrayal

I have thought about Peter and Judas. Both failed the Lord, but only one recovered. In my opinion, Peter and Judas were the two main apostles. You may question my assumption about Judas, however, consider the fact that Judas was the treasurer. You do not place a novice over such an important job, rather someone you can trust. Judas was made faithful over the money and I believe he was in line to be the chief apostle.

What caused him to betray Christ? These passages give us the real reason: *But one of his disciples, Judas Iscariot, who was later to betray him, objected, "Why wasn't this perfume sold and the money given to the poor? It was worth a year's wages." He did not say this because he cared about the poor but because he was a thief; as keeper of the money bag, he used to help himself to what was put into it. "Leave her alone," Jesus replied. "It was intended that she should save this perfume for the day of my burial. You will always have the poor among you, but you will not always have me."* (John 12:4-8).

Judas had character flaws, such as dipping into the money bag. Peter, also, had defects, including his pride and anger. Neither were perfect.

The Lord frequently rebuked Peter. "Oh, you, of little faith." "Get thee behind me, Satan." "You will deny me three times." However, we only find Jesus chastising Judas this one time.

What was Judas Thinking?

Unlike Peter's folly, Judas seemed to have a good case. Mary had poured perfume on Jesus that cost a year's wage. Doesn't that sound like waste?

Jesus allowed the expenditure, yet Judas objected.

Let's read another parallel passage about this story that will shed even more light. It gives a greater insight into Judas' thinking. *While he was in Bethany, reclining at the table in the home of a man known as Simon the Leper, a woman came with an alabaster jar of very expensive perfume, made of pure nard. She broke the jar and poured the perfume on his head. Some of those present were saying indignantly to one another, "Why this waste of perfume? It could have been sold for more than a year's wages and the money given to the poor." And they rebuked her harshly. "Leave her alone," said Jesus. "Why are you bothering her? She has done a beautiful thing to me. The poor you will always have with you, and you can help them any time you want. But you will not always have me. She did what she could. She poured perfume on my body beforehand to prepare for my burial. I tell you the truth, wherever the gospel is preached throughout the world, what she has done will also be told, in memory of her"* (Mark 14:3-9).

"Why are you bothering her?"

Perhaps you noticed that Judas is not mentioned in this account. Only that "some of those" rebuked Mary. We know from John's gospel that Judas led the group in their opposition of this wasted perfume.

This reveals what was happening. Judas was being a leader, and he seemed to have a sizable group on his side. It is easy to not see the offense when it appears so many others agree with you. This is also a trick of the enemy since the majority is not always right.

GETTING EVEN

Not only did Jesus rebuke Judas, He scolded him in front of the others. That was no doubt embarrassing, but then again, Jesus admonished Peter before the disciples many times.

Judas, though, is different. Because he was the treasurer, his opinion was especially valued. If anyone should know how the money should be spent, it was Judas – that was his specialty. Yet, Jesus does not seem impressed with Judas's credentials.

Jesus not only reprimanded Judas in front of his peers, He then adds, "I tell you the truth, wherever the gospel is preached throughout the world, what she has done will also be told, in memory of her." What? This incident will not be kept secret. The whole world will know the real Judas!

We know that his challenger, Peter, was doubtful, prideful and prone to put his foot in his mouth. Yet he survived. In fact, he was proud to tell others of his failures – and that the Lord was a forgiving Master.

Judas was different; he could not take correction. He was indignant that the Lord did not appreciate his opinion. The scolding was too much for him. Notice the next verse: *Then Judas Iscariot, one of the Twelve, went to the chief priests to betray Jesus to them* (Mark 14:10).

It is clear that Judas was so offended he betrayed his Master. I'm sure he rationalized that he was doing Israel a favor. Yet deep inside, the real cause of his betrayal was offense. He was insulted, and now he would get even.

He did! Christ was crucified just as Judas planned.

Unfortunately Judas did not know Satan's plan. Judas never recovered.

An Exceptional Man

What a contrast we see in the life of John the Baptist.

If there ever was a perfect human being other than Christ, it was this disciple. Jesus declared, *Among those born of women there has not risen anyone greater than John the Baptist* (Matthew 11:11).

The Bible paints a portrait of an exceptional man. Could anything tempt him?

John was outspoken, rebuking Herod for taking his brother's wife. His boldness, however, landed him in prison. The news of his arrest spread quickly, yet John was proud that he had suffered for Christ. He was there because of truth.

John took comfort knowing that his cousin, Jesus, was out preaching the gospel. The disciple had been privileged to see the Holy Spirit descend on Christ in the form of a dove – and had testified that Jesus was the Lamb of God who would take away the sins of the world. Since John was in line to be the high priest in Israel, he knew the meaning of the sacrificial role of the "lamb."

Instead of waiting to be ordained as high priest, he heard God's call to go into the desert. There he met the real Lamb of God. As a faithful high priest, he reluctantly laid hands on Christ and baptized him into a watery grave. This was a preview of the scene of sacrifice when Christ would become the Lamb that was slain.

Where was Jesus?

Now John was in prison, and began to wonder what

Jesus was doing. Word was spreading over the country about this Miracle-worker. Then the thought struck him, "I'm sure Jesus has heard that I am in prison and will visit me shortly. Sure he is busy, but I'm his cousin."

John waited and waited – for days, weeks, then months. "Where is Jesus? Surely He has not forgotten me!" John must have worried.

He could take it no longer. John sent two of his own disciples to ask Jesus if He was truly the Messiah, or should they look for another. Do you notice a tinge of resentment? Jesus had never visited him. Now he questions his own visions and revelations. Maybe Jesus is not the One after all. Perhaps John had been deceived.

"Surely He has not forgotten me!"

John's disciples found that Jesus was busy praying for people, occupied by teaching the Word of God to the hungry. Finally, John's disciples interrupted: *Are you the one who was to come, or should we expect someone else?* (Matthew 11:3).

Jesus knew their hearts and did not give them a straight answer. He replied, *Go back and report to John what you hear and see: The blind receive sight, the lame walk, those who have leprosy are cured, the deaf hear, the dead are raised, and the good news is preached to the poor* (vv.4-5).

HE REPENTED

The disciples must have looked puzzled. Was that a "yes" or "no"? They bowed their heads and turned. As they were walking away, Jesus added a personal message for John, *And blessed is he, whosoever shall not be offended in me* (v.6 KJV).

That seemed a strange statement. The disciples must have asked themselves, "What did He mean by that?" When they arrived at the prison, John asked them what Jesus had said and they gave him the word about Jesus healing and preaching. They left out the message concerning offense.

Finally, John forces them, "Is there anything else He said?" Reluctantly the disciples answered, "Well...yes. He said, 'Blessed is he who is not offended in me.'"

John's eyes fell. Yet he could see more clearly than ever before – he had been ensnared by the devil and did not know it. John had been trapped. He was *offended*, and Jesus revealed his true heart.

The physical prison was nothing compared to his spirit being confined. Unlike Judas, John quickly repented.

How about you, can you see the offense in your life? Someone has harmed you. You don't want to go to church anymore. You don't want to face the people who hurt you. Be honest. You are trapped!

Will you be like John and repent, or be like Judas and die with bitterness in your heart? *An offended brother is more unyielding than a fortified city, and disputes are like the barred gates of a citadel* (Proverbs 18:19).

Resentment is difficult to heal. Those who possess it feel betrayed and become unyielding. In some ways there is more hope for a heroine addict than for an offended brother.

"You don't understand. They were wrong and I'm right!" you insist. Do you want to be *right* or do you want to be *free*? The choice is yours.

LET IT GO!

It's time to break loose from Satan's power. Don't hold

onto your right to be *right*. Forgive. Let the bitterness go. Pardon whoever hurt you or let you down. We are all human. Who are you to judge your brother?

Offer this prayer to the Lord?

> *Father, I see that I am caught in Satan's trap. I need your help. I have allowed the enemy to magnify the sins of my brothers and sisters. I'm so sorry for letting offense trap me. I forgive anyone that I think has done me wrong. And more importantly, I ask you to forgive me for my foolishness. I free myself from the snare of the enemy. I have come to my senses. I see the truth. I will walk in forgiveness and peace with my family.*
>
> *In Jesus name I pray, Amen!*

Let Satan say about you, "He was the big fish that got away!"

Part IV

The Evidence

Chapter 14

The Power Encounter

I have a deep-seated concern for the body of Christ. If *anyone* should know the power of Satan and the need to drive him and his cohorts out of the lives of people, it should be the church. Yet there is much skepticism concerning the need for deliverance.

The Catholic Church, it is reported, performs less than a dozen exorcisms a year. What about Protestant churches? They have traditionally shunned the supernatural - and many view demons as figments of people's imaginations. It seems that the "age of reason" has destroyed the Protestant church's ability to see the need for deliverance.

There is a glimmer of hope on the horizon. Some evangelicals are finally trying to press into this needed ministry, yet they often fall short of embracing the necessity for power encounters for Christians. They admit that demons are real and will leave people when they come to Christ for salvation. However, experience tells us that demons often do not completely depart when people are born again.

No doubt, salvation is the *beginning* of deliverance, but the born-again experience is not the *end* of the process.

There is much in the Bible to prove that demons can influence Christians and that they need to stay vigilant against the devil. Of course, unbelievers also need deliverance, but until they come to Christ, any results will be short-lived.

Fortunately, of late, evangelicals are coming to the realization that even Christians may be demonized. They are not *possessed* – because the Lord lives in the believer. We use the term *demonized* to indicate they are influenced or controlled to a certain extent by demons.

SHEDDING LIGHT

The bestselling book, *The Bondage Breaker* by Neil T. Anderson has brought the evangelical community a great distance from its *dinosauric* ways in which they used to view demons as being huddled in third-world countries where natives practice voodoo.

Anderson brought the need for deliverance into the pew – and even to the pulpit. The book was a surprising success! Baptists, Methodists and Bible-believing denominations accepted its message. Yet with all the good that resulted from his writing, I do believe it fell short of bringing the evangelicals to fully embrace the need for a full-blown deliverance ministry. Even the author admits, "I have not attempted to 'cast out a demon' in several years. But I have seen hundreds of people find freedom in Christ as I helped them resolve their personal and spiritual conflicts. I no longer deal directly with demons at all, and I prohibit their manifestation."

A TRUTH ENCOUNTER?

I am delighted for the hundreds that have been helped through counseling alone. I believe they truly benefitted, yet for Anderson to say that he has "not attempted to cast out a demon in several years" is not helping the church accept deliverance.

The reason for his methodology is based on his view of a *truth encounter* verses a *power encounter*. He writes: "We have mistakenly regarded freedom as the product of a power encounter instead of a truth encounter. We must avoid buying into Satan's second strategy of power as much as we avoid swallowing his first strategy of deception. It isn't power per se that sets the captive free; it's *truth* (John 8:32)."

Anderson sees only the need for truth encounters, perceiving power encounters as blasé or perhaps even hurtful. He also believes that people need simply to hear the Word, and the Word alone will cure people from demons.

I am an avid believer in the power of God's Word to set people free, and have witnessed that the truth liberates those in bondage. Yet I have also seen the need to use the power of the Holy Spirit to directly drive out demons.

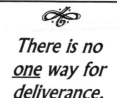

> ***There is no <u>one</u> way for deliverance.***

I don't believe, as Anderson does, that truth encounters have made power encounters obsolete. I believe in both methods. Just as Jesus healed in a variety of ways, there is no *one* way for deliverance. Sometimes the spoken Word is sufficient, other times prayer is needed, and still other times deliverance is required.

What Does Jesus Say?

I believe you have learned from the book you are now reading that God provides various solutions for different illnesses – and that the truth can bring liberty.

Healing Through Deliverance has been based on breaking bondage through the power of the Word. Since I am not physically present with you, I believe it can provide the answers you need.

However, if we were meeting face to face I would couple the teaching of the Word with prayer for deliverance. They both work effectively.

It is not my opinion or Anderson's that count. Study scripture, especially the words of Jesus regarding deliverance. He declared, *But if I drive out demons by the Spirit of God, then the kingdom of God has come upon you* (Matthew 12:28).

How did the Lord drive out demons? By the *spirit of God.* Certainly the Holy Spirit inspired the Bible, yet Jesus did not mean that He drove out the spirits by using the Bible. He meant the *power* of the Holy Spirit.

In another gospel Jesus' words are expressed this way: *But if I drive out demons by the finger of God, then the kingdom of God has come to you* (Luke 11:20).

The *finger of God* is the Holy Spirit. It does not take a huge surge of energy to drive out demons, simply God's touch. Satan flees not solely because of truth, but by divine power. This is how the Apostles drove out demons: *When Jesus had called the Twelve together, he gave them power and authority to drive out all demons and to cure diseases* (Luke 9:1).

It was through a *power encounter!*

The apostles would not agree with Mr. Anderson's

recommendation not to engage in power encounters with demons. I am more than disappointed in the writer's conclusions, and what grieves me more is that he sees such confrontations as "buying into Satan's...strategy."

I believe it is a *lack* of power that causes people to adopt the devil's agenda.

Regardless of how people may judge me, I choose to drive out demons the way Jesus and the apostles did - directly through power encounters.

WHY CHURCHES AVOID DELIVERANCE

I have thought intensely about the possible reasons churches shy away from directly confronting Satan when deliverance is needed. I know it is not the Word of God that makes them hesitate. Scripture clearly advocates a bold approach.

So what is behind the decision to keep the church from exercising its dynamic power? There are basically four reasons:

> ***"I feel uncomfortable with such emotional outbursts."***

1. They dislike emotional outbursts.

Let's face it. Power encounters can be an unusual sight - someone falling on the floor, screaming, crying, swinging their arms. For conservative people, this kind of confrontation goes against their grain. One man said, "I feel uncomfortable with such emotional outbursts."

Many prefer religious gatherings to be composed and

orderly. They don't understand that demons are often noisy and *loud*.

To shy away from dealing with Satan because of the personality of a congregation runs contrary to the nature of God. Can we dictate how He wants to work?

Can we dictate how He wants to work?

I encourage people who are reserved to get over their personal objections to the ministry of deliverance. Recognize that this work is needed and is biblical. When we come to a full understanding I believe we will accept it.

There are individuals in our church who are quiet in nature – yet, despite their personality, they have learned to welcome the workings of God.

2. They are afraid to cause trauma in the candidate for deliverance.

There are some who have genuine concern that the ministry of deliverance may do more harm than good. They are afraid to bring emotional trauma to the individual by driving out demons.

This is a legitimate concern, yet remember God's ways are always best. He would never tell us to drive out demons if people would be hurt in the process.

There is no evidence that deliverance causes injury. Just the contrary. Psychological studies, as well as my own personal experience, have proven that people receive positive benefits through the prayer of deliverance. They testify to feeling better, drawing closer to God, and feeling that they can handle everyday problems with strength.

Of course, I am aware of those who have gone off the deep end concerning this type of ministry. I have heard horror stories of people being held against their will while biblically illiterate individuals prayed for them.

If someone refuses prayer, I respect their decision. I am not going to force my prayers on anyone.

There are also rare cases where people have actually *beaten* the demonized. God does not need anyone to use physical force to drive out demons.

3. They are skeptical of miracles.

Once, when the disciples failed to drive out a demon from a young boy (Mark 9:14-32), Jesus asked, "Why do you doubt?"

Lack of faith is still the number one reason people abstain from a deliverance ministry.

Let's be honest and admit that many question the supernatural. Even Christians are wary of demons. They know the Bible mentions them, but they rationalize those verses – thinking it refers to the superstitious thinking of the people in Bible days.

Well, if Jesus drove out demons, was He superstitious? Many people of faith want to believe in Jesus, yet they overlook His ministry of deliverance. They often seem *embarrassed* concerning it. Doubt has overridden their faith.

The Bible tell us, *So then faith cometh by hearing, and hearing by the word of God* (Romans 10:17).

The only way people will eliminate their uncertainty is to keep hearing the Word of God on this subject. It is one of the primary reasons I have written this book.

4. They always want permanent results.

Many in the clergy have shunned away from this topic

because they often see the lack of permanent results in people when they are delivered.

Some even had a deliverance ministry, but became frustrated when they saw people return to their sin or sickness. Without doubt, it can be discouraging when an individual does not maintain his or her healing.

I have felt the same way. However, I do not give up this ministry because people do not keep their deliverance anymore than I would stop preaching the gospel of salvation simply because people return to their ungodly ways.

I do not see marriage counselors closing their doors because some couples divorce after claiming to have been helped.

Jesus told us that demons would try to return to make matters worse. Thus, it should not surprise us when some people do not stay delivered.

The marvelous news, however, is that many *do* keep their deliverance. We need to rejoice with those who continue to walk in liberty and freedom.

IT'S BIBLICAL!

Whatever may be your reason for shying away from dealing with Satan and his demons, I pray you will look again at the Word. I believe you will come to the conclusion there are no scriptural grounds for staying out of the deliverance ministry.

It is biblical, and it works!

CHAPTER 15

REAL STORIES OF DELIVERANCE

Many people, including reporters, have asked me, "Does deliverance really work?" They want evidence.

Let me share a few stories from people I know personally – members of our church – who received their healing when they were delivered from evil spirits.

SANDRA CARRASCO

A wife and mother of two, Sandra Carrasco was married to Arturo, a successful businessman in the community. Everything seemed happy with this couple, yet Sandra was acting anything but normal.

For no apparent reason, thoughts were whirling in her mind – "You have nothing to live for. Just end your life!"

One day, as this was taking place, Sandra grabbed her keys and took off frantically in the car. Her intention was to drive to the nearby mountains and ride her vehicle off one of the cliffs.

She sped out of her driveway and zigged in and out of the traffic lanes, determined to end her life. Suddenly, she noticed another car following closely behind. It would mimic her driving. She attempted to dodge it, but the driver persisted. Although the car was behind her, it seemed that it was guiding her path. Finally she turned into a church parking lot. The car vanished.

I picked up the phone and could tell immediately that Sandra was distraught.

Afraid and exhausted, she thought, "What am I going to do? I need to call my pastor." So she frantically dialed my house.

I picked up the phone and could tell immediately that Sandra was distraught. She did not sound like herself and, concerned, I told her to drive to our house – even though she had not been there before.

I learned later that just before she hung up she heard me say our street name. It somehow stuck in her mind.

As she left the church parking lot, she drove down Montwood Drive, and to her surprise there was our street. She passed it, made a U-turn and drove back, looking for my car. *There it was!* She stopped and walked to my door, still in a daze.

My wife, Sonia, and I invited her in and immediately began to ask questions. She confessed that she wanted to end her life. We gave her some encouragement, but quickly realized that her condition was not normal – I felt there were demons that were oppressing her.

Sandra was seated on our couch and Sonia stood next to her side. I then proceeded to lay my hands on her head and commanded every demon to leave her life. When I did, Sandra began to scream. The demons were yelling through her, "No!"

Sandra slid down the couch, lying on her back. I was praying over her, still commanding the demons to leave.

A battle was raging in her soul.

A battle was raging in her soul. Her hands were violently flailing back and forth, but not once was my wife or I hit. God protected us from any physical harm.

After ten minutes, the demons departed. Sandra came out of the daze and a wide smile broke across her face. She knew without a doubt she was delivered!

This took place nearly ten years ago. Sandra Carrasco became one of the deacons in our church.

MY MOTHER

It was an embarrassing secret. For more than twenty years my mother, Billie, was too ashamed to admit that she had hidden her disease of bulimia from the family.

During those years she had regularly vomited her food. This was her way of controlling her weight, but in reality, the condition was controlling her.

Professionals tell us that there is no real cure for this disease. The best they can hope for is for patients to make a decision to decrease their vomiting.

However, God can heal the disease completely.

Our church was meeting in a rented facility at the time

my mother came forward for prayer. I remember feeling especially anointed that Sunday – and boldness was on me in an extraordinary way.

I called for people to come forward who needed the Lord to deliver them. To my surprise, of the three who walked to the front, my mother was one of them.

I thought, "What does she need deliverance from?" Yet in he eyes I could see desperation turn to tears.

I thought, "What does she need deliverance from?" Yet in her eyes I could see desperation turn to tears.

As I prayed, my mother began to shake uncontrollably, letting out a few gasps. Then she felt an awful presence leave her body. "Could that be a demon?" she wondered. We now know it was – and praise God, she was free!

This took place several years ago, and my mother has never suffered the symptoms of bulimia since.

Healing came through deliverance.

BRENDA CABALLERO

It was Monday, October 29, 2001. The weather was turning cold in El Paso, yet that wasn't the reason Brenda Caballero felt chills that evening.

Her father, Guillermo, had come home drunk. That wasn't unusual, but what was about to happen certainly was.

He had finished eating supper and went to his room to

watch TV. Brenda told him, "Dad, you need to get some rest. Turn off the television and go to sleep."

Immediately, Guillermo became angry. "Leave me alone!," her father shouted. He was going through some family problems, so his daughter was sympathetic and left the room.

Brenda was in her bedroom when she heard a thud. Then she listened as her father yelled, "Satan, come into my soul!"

She could not believe her ears! Running into his bedroom, she could see that her father seemed "out of it," yet he was wide awake.

Brenda found the family Bible, wiped off the dust and began to read from the book of Psalms.

The demon began to audibly rage against Brenda, "Get out the room. Leave us alone. We don't want to hear that junk!"

She refused to listen to the demon's orders and continued to read. Her father quickly jumped out of the bed and knocked the Bible out of her hands. "I don't want you to read," he bellowed. "I want to watch TV!"

"I don't want you to read," he bellowed. "I want to watch TV."

So Brenda obliged and turned on the television to the Christian channel. On the screen was *Good News El Paso,* the media ministry of our church.

I was preaching about the power of *good* – and how it will defeat evil. I declared, "God is your strength. You do not need to fear!"

As Brenda was watching the program, she lifted her

hands and asked for God's strength to help her father. At that moment her father screamed, "Change the channel. We don't want to hear that preacher!"

This time Brenda defiantly stood up to the demon and began to fervently pray for her father. The more she prayed, the more her father cursed. He would cover his ears, "We don't want to hear you pray! Stop!"

He stood up and walked to the restroom. As he did, Brenda noticed huge scratches on his back.

He fell to the floor, cursing and covering his ears.

Guillermo cried to his daughter and said, "There is a demon inside of me!"

She hugged and assured him everything was going to be all right. As she began to pray again, the demon, once more began to swear through her father. He fell to the floor, cursing and covering his ears.

Brenda said with authority, "In the name of Jesus, I order you, the demon in my father, to leave his body and return to hell!"

As she uttered those words, the demon left him with a loud shriek and a hideous gurgle sound. Her father began to sob and hugged his daughter – he thanked her for helping him. Guillermo, because of his drunken condition, still does not remember everything that happened that night.

After this incident they began faithfully attending our church.

WHAT ABOUT YOU?

There are many similar testimonies in our congregation.

I have included these few as an encouragement for you to find your own freedom in Christ.

What I have learned through the Word and personal experience is that deliverance is a divine key to miracles.

Allow God to work in your life and let Him uncover any evil that may be hidden within. Like a silversmith who scoops up the dross when the metal is hot, God will remove every evil force so that you will be set free.

There is healing through deliverance.

ACKNOWLEDGMENTS

There are always many people to thank when a book is published. First, I am grateful to our church members for allowing me to share the revelation of this book. I knew from your receptivity that the message was life-changing.

Thanks to my proofreaders: Shirleen Ledoux, Sue Mitchell and Fernie Rodriguez. I appreciate your invaluable suggestions. And a big thank you goes to Neil Eskelin at LifeBridge Books for believing in this project.

To my children, Justin, Faith and Caleb who think I spend too much time on the computer – you see, I really *am* working.

And how could I ever forget the wife of my youth. Thank you, Sonia, for always encouraging me and providing your personal insights in order to improve this book.

Of course, without the Lord, how could I ever accomplish anything? Thank you, Lord, for counting me faithful in service to You. The worst day in ministry is better than the best day in the world!

For a Complete list of Books,
Tapes and Videos by Tom Brown

Contact:

Tom Brown Ministries
P.O. Box 27275
El Paso, TX 79926

Phone: 915-857-0962
Internet: www.tbm.org
Email: tom@tbm.org